The 401(k)/403(b) Investment Manual

What Plan Participants and Plan Sponsors
<u>REALLY</u> Need to Know

InvestSense, LLC

Let's make a dent in the universe.

Steve Jobs

Table of Contents

Introduction

America's 401(k), 403(b), and 457(b) retirement plans are a mess. It has been estimated that the 2008 bear market resulted in investment losses in the trillions of dollars for investors, with a large part of those losses undoubtedly occurring in retirement accounts. Many of those losses in retirement accounts might have been avoided had the plan itself been structured properly and plan participants been provided with meaningful and effective investment information and education programs.

As a former investment compliance professional, I am all too aware of some of the issues, ethical and otherwise, involved with the financial services industry's marketing of retirement plans to corporations, schools, hospitals and governmental organizations, issues that often end up hurting plan participants. As a securities and wealth preservation attorney, as well as both a CERTIFIED FINANCIAL PLANNER™ professional and an ACCREDITED WEALTH MANAGEMENT ADVISOR℠ professional, I help people address those issues and become proactive in managing their investments, showing them how to avoid those issues as they pursue their financial goals.

When I do a prudence analysis or a forensic portfolio analysis for a retirement plan or an individual investor, I use a number of analytical tools, including the InvestSense™ Ratio, a proprietary formula that allows me to analyze the efficiency of an investment, both in terms of risk and cost. While the information discussed herein is neither intended to allow, nor will allow, a plan participant or a plan sponsor to perform the in-depth analysis that I perform, the information has been provided in hopes of helping plan sponsors in spotting questionable marketing tactics and helping plan participants in creating and maintaining cost-efficient and effectively diversified retirement portfolios.

Financial education is an ongoing process. One of my favorite quotes is that of Thomas Jefferson, who stated that "knowledge is power, knowledge is protection, knowledge is happiness." I am also a firm believer in the truth contained in the legend on my "CommonSense InvestSense" blog, "The Power of the Informed Investor." I invite you to visit my blog and to continue the investment education process in order to protect your financial security.

Chapter One

A Curious Paradox

Common sense is not that common
Voltaire

In 1974, Congress passed the Employee Retirement Income Security Act (ERISA).[1] ERISA was enacted to protect employees and their retirement accounts. Three primary themes appear consistently throughout ERISA: disclosure of important information, diversification of investments to protect against large losses, and cost control to avoid unnecessary fees and expenses.

Not all retirement plans are subject to ERISA's regulations. The two most notable exemptions from ERISA are governmental plans and church plans, commonly referred to as 403(b) and 457(b) plans. While it is possible for both governmental and church plans to become subject to ERISA's regulations, they are generally exempt from such regulations.

When people think of retirement plans, they often think in terms of 401(k) plans. 401(k) plans are the most common type of retirement plans offered by corporations and other business entities. 401(k) plans are referred to as defined contribution plans, meaning that the primary source of funding is through employee contributions to their individual accounts. Employers may match an employee's contributions up to a certain amount; however, such employer contributions are not required. In order to reduce potential liability, many employers have chosen to convert their 401(k) plans into so-called 404(c) retirement plans. 404(c) plans are commonly referred to as "participant-directed" plans since each participant is responsible for selecting, monitoring and managing the investments in their account.

If an employer complies with all of ERISA section 404(c)'s requirements, then the employer will generally not be held responsible for any losses that a plan participant suffers in their 404(c) account. However, ERISA section 404(c) does not relieve a plan sponsor for liability in connection with their duty to continue to monitor the investment alternatives to ensure that the investment options remain prudent for the plan.

401(k) sponsors and others have expressed concerns that employees may not have sufficient investment experience and/or knowledge to properly manage their investments. This concern is supported by a recent Securities and Exchange Commission study which concluded that most American investors are financially illiterate.[2] Making matters even worse is the fact that while ERISA allows employers to shift the risk of investment losses to their employees, ERISA does not require employers to provide any type of investment education or investment advice to employees.

In 2012, I posted a white paper on one of my blogs. The white paper, entitled " A Curious Paradox: Reconciling MPT and ERISA Section 404(c)'s 'Informed Decision' Requirement to Protect Plan Fiduciaries and Participants", dealt with the apparent inconsistency between the prudence requirements established by the Department of Labor and the courts and the disclosure requirements under section 404(c).

One of the requirements for ERISA section 404(c) status is that an employer provides each plan participant with "sufficient information to make an informed decision as to each investment alternative offered."[3] Both the Department of Labor and the courts have established that in assessing the prudence of a fiduciary's acts under ERISA, the principles established by Modern Portfolio Theory (MPT) are the appropriate standards of review. [4]

MPT was first introduced by Dr. Harry Markowitz in 1952.[5] Prior to the introduction of MPT, investment portfolios were constructed on the basis of an investment's risk and return alone. With the introduction of MPT, Markowitz introduced the concept of including the correlation of returns between investments in the portfolio construction process, the rationale being that the risk of large investment losses can be reduced by combining assets with low, or even negative, correlations of return.

While MPT has been the subject of legitimate criticism in terms of its calculation process, the concept of factoring in the correlation of returns between investments as part of the portfolio construction process has proven to be both viable and valuable for investors. Given the fact that the importance of considering the correlation of returns between investments has been acknowledged by both the Department of Labor and the courts, the failure of the Department of Labor or ERISA to require that such information be provided to ERISA plan participants is puzzling.

The cumulative effect of the failure of either the Department of Labor or ERISA to require that retirement plan participants be provided with correlation of returns data, as well as the failure to require that plan participants be provided with investment education and investment advice, leaves plan participants vulnerable to unnecessary investment losses, unnecessary investment costs, and, in some cases, investment fraud. This continuing paradox is both unnecessary and clearly inconsistent with ERISA's announced purpose and goal of protecting retirement plan participants.

Chapter Two

Fiduciary Duties Under ERISA

Not honesty alone, but the punctilio of an honor the most sensitive, is then the standard of behavior [for fiduciaries].
Justice Benjamin Cardozo

Generally speaking, ERISA requires a fiduciary to carry out their duties to their plan "solely in the best interest of the participants and beneficiaries."[1] ERISA sets out four general duties for a fiduciary, namely

- A duty of loyalty – a duty to act for the exclusive purpose of providing benefits to plan participants and their beneficiaries;

- A duty of prudence – a duty to act "with the care, skill, prudence and diligence under the circumstances then prevailing that a prudent man acting in a like capacity and familiar with such matters would use in the conduct of an enterprise of a like character and with like aims";

- A duty to diversify – a duty to diversify the plan's investments "so as to minimize the risk of large losses, unless under the circumstances it is clearly prudent not to do so"; and

- A duty of compliance – a duty to "administer the plan in accordance with [the governing] documents and instruments" to the extent that such documents and instruments are consistent with ERISA's requirements."[2]

An ERISA fiduciary has a number of disclosure duties, particularly with regard to information pertaining to a plan's investment alternatives. If an ERISA plan elects to seek 404(c) status, the plan's fiduciaries have an even greater duty of disclosure given the fact that the burden of investment management and liability for any investment losses is shifted to plan participants. The fiduciary duty of disclosure will be discussed in more detail in Chapter 5.

Chapter Three

A Battle of the Best Interests

*It is difficult to get a man to understand something when
his salary depends upon his not understanding it.*
Upton Sinclair

*The typical fund company services [401(k) plan] participants
in the same way that Baby Face Nelson serviced banks.*
William Bernstein

Under ERISA, a plan's fiduciaries are required to always put the interests of the plan's participants first. As one court stated, ERISA's fiduciary duties "are the highest known to law,"[1] and "a pure heart and an empty head are no defense"[2] to breaches of ERISA fiduciary duties.

One plan fiduciary duty is to control a plan's costs and to avoid unnecessary expenses. One cost cutting strategy often used by ERISA fiduciaries is to allow so-called plan providers to have access to plan participants in exchange for the plan providers providing administrative services to the plan.

Plan fiduciaries often attempt to justify these arrangements by pointing out that these administrative services can often be costly to a plan and that such costs would reduce the participants' investment returns if the plan had to pay for such services. What plan fiduciaries do not mention is that ERISA allows the employer or other plan sponsor to pay for such costs.

Even more important, these access arrangements often cost plan participants disproportionately more than their proportionate share of any administrative fees, both in terms of costs and investment returns. Recent regulations have been enacted by the Department of Labor in hopes of providing plan fiduciaries and plan participants with greater transparency regarding a plan's fees and other investment expenses.[3]

While the new regulations may provide greater insight into the impact of investment fees and other expenses on a plan participant's investment returns, the Department of Labor and other regulatory bodies need to address the quality of investments offered under such access agreements and the quality of investment education programs and investment advice often offered as part of these agreements. Far too often the plan providers take advantage of the situation and offer a poor selection of investment alternatives for the plan participants.

The problem with plan provider access agreements is that they necessarily involve a battle of the best interests, a battle which too often results in plan participants losing the battle. While ERISA plan fiduciaries have an obligation to control costs, ERISA fiduciaries also have an even higher duty to always act in the best interests of the plan participants and their beneficiaries. Therefore, plan fiduciaries must also conduct a meaningful cost-benefit analysis of the proposed access agreement, involving both a cost efficiency and an investment performance analysis, prior to approving an agreement with any outside third party.

Unfortunately, there is evidence that such an analysis is not happening in many cases. Far too often it appears that plan fiduciaries are just blindly accepting whatever plan providers are offering them without proper consideration and/or evaluation of the potential costs to the plan participants, both in terms of fees/expenses and investment performance.

In some cases it is because the plan fiduciary does not have the experience or knowledge to properly evaluate such agreements. Sadly, in other cases, a proper analysis of an access agreement may not be performed due to the payment of illegal monetary incentives between plan fiduciaries and plan providers.

Whatever the reason, the takeaway for plan participants is the need to be proactive in managing their retirement accounts. Plan participants need to evaluate both the quality of the investment alternatives offered by a plan and the fees involved in order to maximize the potential benefits of their plan and, in some instances, to improve their plan.

Chapter Four

Fiduciary "Trickeration"

Appearances are often deceiving.
Aesop

Retirement plans often use consultants to help them manage the plan. From a fiduciary standpoint, there are basically three types of retirement plan consultants: the consultant who denies any fiduciary responsibility whatsoever; the ERISA 3(38) fiduciary, or investment manager, who accepts full fiduciary responsibility and liability for the services that the fiduciary provides to the plan; and the ERISA 3(21) fiduciary, who generally provides a more limited scope of fiduciary services and, therefore, accepts a more limited scope of fiduciary responsibility and liability.

The first two types of consultants are pretty straightforward. The 3(21) ERISA fiduciary can be more problematic for both the plan sponsor and plan participants. In defining an ERISA 3(21) fiduciary, ERISA states that a person is a fiduciary with respect to a plan to the extent

- he exercises any discretionary authority or discretionary control respecting management of such plan or exercises any authority or control respecting management or disposition of its assets,
- he renders investment advice for a fee or other compensation, direct or indirect, with respect to any moneys or other property of such plan, or has any authority or responsibility to do so, or
- he has any discretionary authority or discretionary responsibility in the administration of such plan.[1]

A closer examination of the requirements for being deemed an ERISA 3(21) fiduciary shows that the two primary requirements are discretionary authority/control or investment advice for a fee with regard to the assets of the plan. Without the presence of one of those requirements, an alleged ERISA 3(21) fiduciary does not meet ERISA's definition of a ERISA 3(21) fiduciary.

Therefore, the consultant arguably has no fiduciary responsibilities or liabilities with regard to either the plan or the plan's participants..

"Trickeration" has been defined as "cunning deception."[2] Savvy plan providers are well aware of ERISA section 3(21)'s "loopholes." Many plan providers deliberately draft their ERISA consulting agreements in such a way as to allow them to hold themselves out to plans as fiduciaries, while at the same time including language within their agreements that effectively prevents them from having any fiduciary responsibilities or liabilities whatsoever to a plan or the plan participants.

Far too often plan sponsors blindly rely on a plan provider's use of the "fiduciary" term without carefully reviewing the terms of the consulting agreement itself. A plan provider can avoid both the designation and the liability of an ERISA 3(21) fiduciary by simply stating that it agrees to serve as an ERISA 3(21) fiduciary to the extent that the services that they agree to provide are covered under ERISA section 3(21). Since ERISA section 3(21) requires that a consultant have either discretionary authority/control or provide investment advice regarding the plan's assets, the plan provider simply includes explicit language in their consulting agreement stating that they will neither have such powers nor provide such services.

To further avoid the possibility of being held liable as an ERISA 3(21) fiduciary, the plan provider's consulting agreement often includes language limiting the plan provider's services to the provision of recommendations regarding money managers, as ERISA section 3(21) only covers advice on investments. To further remove any questions of control and liability, the plan provider's consulting agreement usually states, often in bold type, that the decision to adopt or reject the plan provider's recommendations is solely the responsibility of the plan.

An example of a plan provider's ERISA 3(21) exculpatory language in their consulting agreement might read as follows:

> Consultant hereby agrees to serve as an ERISA section 3(21) fiduciary to the extent that the services described herein come within the services set forth by ERISA section 3(21). Consultant and Plan expressly understand and agree that consultant's services hereunder shall be limited to reviewing and evaluating money managers and providing recommendations on money managers to the Plan.

Consultant and Plan expressly understand and agree that the decision as to whether to adopt or reject any or all of Consultant's recommendations, in whole or in part, shall be the sole responsibility of the Plan. Consultant and Plan expressly understand and agree that under no circumstance shall Consultant assume or accept discretionary power over the Plan or its assets or provide investment advice with regard to the investment alternatives for or within the Plan.

Net result, the plan provider can claim to be a fiduciary to the plan. However, in reality, as long as the plan provider's consulting agreement is properly drafted, the plan provider has no fiduciary responsibilities or liabilities to the plan and the plan's sponsor retains sole fiduciary responsibility and liability to the plan and the plan's participants.

But the fiduciary trickeration does not end there. Plan sponsors often decide to allow the plan providers to provide educational programs to the plan participants. After all, the plan provider is supposedly a fiduciary to the plan, so plan sponsors assume that the plan provider can be trusted to provide quality information to the plan's participants.

Once again, plan providers can provide services to the plan and the plan participants without having to assume any fiduciary responsibilities or liabilities. Recognizing both the need and the value of investment education programs for plan participants, the Department of Labor has adopted regulations that allow plans to provide certain types of investment education programs and investment advice without having to be concerned about resulting fiduciary liability.

For educational programs to be truly meaningful, they must provide objective, meaningful and timely information. Unfortunately, such is often not the case when a plan's educational programs are being provided by the plan providers, who are usually trying to promote the investment platform that they convinced the plan sponsor to adopt. In such cases, concerns about inherent biases and conflicts of interest must naturally exist.

In my experience, most plan-provided educational programs consist of a PowerPoint presentation extolling the value of diversification and the presentation of various multi-colored pie charts suggesting model portfolios for the plan participants. Interestingly enough, such programs often fail to discuss the fact that the investment alternatives that the plan provider convinced the plan to adopt are not necessarily in the best interests of the plan or the plan's participants due to the high correlation of returns between the investment alternatives and the overall cost inefficiency of the investments offered by the plan, two topics that will be covered more fully later on.

For the time being, it is enough that both plan participants and plan sponsors understand and appreciate the potential harm that can come from fiduciary trickeration, particularly with regard to plan providers claiming to be ERISA section 3(21) fiduciaries. With regard to ERISA section 3(21) fiduciaries, the best advice for both plan participants and plan sponsors might be found in the admonition that "a little skepticism never hurt anyone," and Ronald Reagan's warning to "trust, but verify."

Chapter Five

Disclosure, Disclosure, Disclosure

Sunlight is the best disinfectant.
Justice Louis Brandeis

Like 404(c) plans, 403(b) and 457(b) plans are participant-directed retirement plans. However, since most 403(b) and 457(b) plans are generally exempt from ERISA's requirements, we will focus on 404(c) participant-directed plans in discussing the disclosure requirements under ERISA. As was mentioned earlier, the required disclosures may not actually be sufficient to allow a plan participant to effectively manage their retirement account.

A plan participant needs to always remember that for 401(k) and 404(c) plans, the overriding disclosure requirement is that the participant or beneficiary "is provided or has the opportunity to obtain sufficient information to make informed investment decisions with regard to investment alternatives available under the plan."[1] A failure to meet, and to continue to meet, this requirement means that the plan and all ERISA fiduciaries of the plan face unlimited personal liability for any and all losses suffered by the plan participants, even losses on investments chosen by the participants.

A complete discussion of the specific statutory disclosure requirements under ERISA is beyond the scope of this book, but those requirements generally include the duty to provide participants with: (1) a summary plan description; (2) a summary annual report; (3) a quarterly benefit statements; and, (4) upon request, various documents and instruments governing the plan.[2]

ERISA requires that certain investment information be automatically provided to plan participants, including:

- Identifying Information - This information consists of the name and investment type or category (e.g., money market fund, balanced fund, large-cap stock fund, employer stock fund, employer securities) of each designated investment alternative.

- Performance Data - This category requires different information for fixed and variable return investments. For variable return investments, the required information consists of the average annual total return for one, five, and ten calendar year periods ending on the most recently completed calendar year. A statement must also be included indicating that an investment's past performance is not necessarily an indication of how the investment will perform in the future.

- Benchmarks - The plan fiduciary must provide plan participants with the name and returns of an appropriate broad-based securities market index over the same one, five, and ten calendar year periods as the performance data periods.

- Fee and Expense Information - The fee and expense information required to be disclosed depends on whether the investment is a variable return or fixed return investment. For variable return investments, the required information includes: the amount and a description of any shareholder-type fees; the total annual operating expenses expressed both as a percentage of assets (i.e., the expense ratio) and as amount for each $1,000 invested; a statement advising plan participants that fees and expenses are only one of several factors that should be considered when making investment decisions; and a statement that the cumulative effect of fees and expenses can substantially reduce the growth of a participant's retirement account and that an example illustrating the impact of such fees and expenses is available at the Department of Labor's EBSA web site.

- Internet Web Site Address - The plan fiduciary is responsible for ensuring the availability of an Internet Web site address that provides additional information for each designated investment option offered by the plan, including: its objectives or goals; its principal strategies (including a general description of the types of assets held by the investment) and risks; the fund's current performance data, updated at least quarterly; and current fee and expense information on the fund.

- Glossary - The plan must furnish either a general glossary of terms to participants and beneficiaries to assist them in understanding the plan' designated investment alternatives, or an Internet web site address that provides access to such a glossary along with a general description of the purpose of that address.[3]

ERISA requires that certain investment information be provided to plan participants upon request, including:

- Copies of prospectuses, or any short form or summary prospectus approved by the Securities and Exchange Commission, disclosing information on investments offered within the plan; and

- Copies of financial statements or reports, such as "statements of additional information" and shareholder reports, and any other similar materials relating to the plan's designated investment alternatives, to the extent that such materials are provided to the plan.[4]

Note the proviso, "to the extent that such materials are provided to the plan." A mutual fund's "Statement of Additional Information" (SAI) often contains important information that an investor should know before investing in the fund. Plan participants should always request and review a copy of a mutual fund's SAI before investing in a mutual fund. If the plan sponsor claims not to have a fund's SAI, then the plan participant should obtain the fund's SAI directly from the fund.

Chapter Six

"Sufficient Information to Make an Informed Decision"

Knowledge is power…knowledge is safety…knowledge is happiness.
Thomas Jefferson

The title of this chapter really summarizes the real issues – what information is really needed by plan participants in order to make a truly informed decision and whether the ERISA plan's sponsor provided such information to plan participants. As mentioned in the last chapter, ERISA requires ERISA fiduciaries to disclose various information to plan participants about both the plan itself and the plan's investment alternatives. Interestingly, some fiduciary disclosures of helpful information are only required if the plan participant actually requests the disclosures.

While ERISA requires certain disclosures regarding a plan's costs and investment alternatives, a case can be made that the information required to be disclosed does not really provide all of the information that plan participants truly need to effectively construct and manage their retirement account. As previously discussed, neither ERISA nor the Department of Labor require ERISA plan fiduciaries to provide plan participants with information regarding the correlation of returns between the investment alternatives offered within the plan. Without such information, plan participants run the risk of constructing a portfolio composed entirely or primarily of highly correlated investments, thereby failing to protect their portfolios with the much needed downside protection against large losses.

Explanations often provided for the failure to provide plan participants with correlation of returns data are often based upon the alleged difficulty in calculating such data and/or the inability of plan participants to understand or use such information. While the correlation of returns data may take a little effort, the data can be calculated with relative ease using the correlation function in Microsoft Excel.

As for the argument that plan participants would not understand or know how to use such information, plan participants could be quickly taught how to interpret and use such data. The old adage, "a picture is worth a thousand words," seems to be especially true with regard to explaining the concept of the correlation of returns to plan participants. A visualization technique using online financial sites has proven to be very successful in helping people understand and utilize correlation of return data.

Using Yahoo!Finance (finance.yahoo.com) as an example, enter a fund's stock market ticker symbol (ticker symbol) in the "Get Quotes" box. In this case enter "VFINX", which is the ticker symbol for the Vanguard 500 Index Investors Fund. Once the page opens, select the "Basic Charts" option in the "Charts" section on the left side of the page.

In the upper half of the page there will be a section marked "Compare." Enter the ticker symbol of the fund that is to be compared to VFINX. For our example, enter "RYURX," which is the ticker symbol for Rydex's Inverse S&P 500 Strategy Fund. Since RYURX is an inverse index fund, we would expect to see a negative correlation of returns between the two funds. Hit the "Compare" button and we see a chart that shows a pattern of returns that are almost opposite images of each other, in other words a low, in this case an almost perfectly negative, correlation of returns.

To see an example of a chart that illustrates what two highly correlated assets looks like, go back to the Yahoo! Finance home page and re-enter the ticker symbol VFINX in the "Quotes" box. Follow the same steps as before, except enter the ticker symbol "VTSMX" in the "Compare" box, VTSMX being the ticker symbol for the Vanguard Total Stock Market Index Fund. Hit the "Compare" button. This time we see a chart that shows a pattern of returns that are almost identical to each other, indicating a high correlation of returns between the two funds.

Plan participants can look up the ticker symbol for the investment alternatives within their retirement plan and use this system to determine the correlation of returns for the alternatives, avoiding a portfolio consisting entirely or primarily of highly correlated investments. By ensuring a portfolio consisting of some investments with a low correlation of returns, a plan participant could provide some protection against suffering large investment losses.

The concept of combining assets that have a low, or even negative, correlation to each other in order to avoid large losses is simply not that hard to understand. Even if a plan participant does not want to learn how to use the correlation of returns data themselves, the information would be useful to advisors that a plan participant might decide to employ.

Both the Department of Labor and the courts have stated that the principles associated with MPT are the applicable standards for assessing the prudence of an ERISA fiduciary's actions, especially with regard to the fiduciary's duty of risk management and diversification. Factoring in the correlation of returns of the investment alternatives being considered is the cornerstone of MPT.

Therefore, in order to meet their duty of prudence, an ERISA fiduciary must factor in the correlation of returns of the investment alternatives that they considered in choosing the plan's investment alternatives. Since the ERISA fiduciary should already have the correlation of returns data for the investment offered within their plan, providing such information to the plan participants should not create a hardship for the plan or the plan's fiduciaries unless the fiduciaries did not obtain and/or consider such correlation of returns data, in which case they have probably violated their fiduciary duty of prudence.

In short, there is no justifiable reason for a 404(c) plan not to provide its participants with correlation of returns data for the investment alternatives offered within the plan. Given the acknowledgement of the importance of such information by both the Department of Labor and the courts, plan participants should be given the same opportunity to use such information to assemble prudent and effectively diversified portfolios in order to protect their financial well-being.

Even though correlation of returns data for investment alternatives within a plan are significant in helping plan participants make informed decisions, cost information is also significant, both in terms of absolute cost and in terms of the benefits derived from such costs. Fees and other costs obviously reduce an investor's end return. A study by the Department of Labor estimated that over a twenty-year period, each 1 percent of fees and other costs will reduce a plan participant's end return by approximately 17 percent.[1]

As previously mentioned, recently enacted regulations require retirement plan sponsors to provide better information to plan participants regarding the fees and other costs associated with the plan, including investments costs. Under the regulations, the information is supposed to be provided in an easy-to-understand format.

Nevertheless, there is justifiable concern over both the accuracy of the information to be provided and its ease of use, especially since no uniform format is required. Since the regulations are relatively new, only time will tell whether these concerns materialize. Early reports are that some reports still appear be cryptic and difficult to interpret.

Even with increased and improved cost disclosure, the disclosures may not fully disclose the impact of such fees on the plan participant's returns. Most investment alternatives within retirement plans are actively managed equity-based mutual funds. Actively managed funds typically have management fees and other costs that are significantly higher than passively managed funds, commonly referred to as index funds.

One aspect of actively managed funds often overlooked is the cost effectiveness of the fund's returns. My company, InvestSense, has developed a simple cost-benefit analysis procedure, the Active Management Value Ratio™, that plan participants can use to determine whether the higher costs associated with an actively managed mutual fund are justified.

To calculate the Active Management Value Ratio™ for an actively managed mutual fund, a plan participant needs to select an appropriate benchmark to use for comparison purposes. Some commonly used benchmarks include the Vanguard S&P 500 Index Fund for large cap funds, the Russell 2000 Index exchange traded fund (ETF) for small cap funds, the MSCI EAFE Index ETF for international equity funds, and the Barclays Capital Aggregate Bond Index ETF for domestic bond funds.

Once an appropriate benchmark has been chosen for each fund being analyzed, a plan participant needs to determine the annual expense ratio and the five-year annualized return for both the actively managed fund and the benchmark fund. I prefer the five-year period, as it is generally more reliable than shorter time periods. I also like to look at rolling return periods to detect aberrations, so five-year periods are easier to work with.

To determine the contribution, if any, of the active management element of a fund, simply subtract the benchmark's annual expense ratio from the actively managed fund's annual expense ratio, and then divide the result by the actively managed fund's annual expense ratio. This provides the active percent component of the actively managed fund's annual expense fee.

For example, assume that the benchmark fund has an annual expense ratio of 0.20 percent and the actively managed fund has an annual expense fee of 1.00 percent. Subtracting the benchmark's annual expense ratio from the actively managed fund's annual expense ratio results in an annual expense ratio balance of 0.80 percent. Dividing the 0.80 percent balance by the actively managed fund's annual expense ratio of 1.00 percent gives us a result of 80 percent, which equals the active management component of the actively managed fund's annual expense ratio.

The next step in computing the Active Management Value Ratio™ is to subtract the benchmark's five-year annualized return from the actively managed fund's five-year annualized return, and then divide the result by the actively managed fund's five-year annualized return. This provides the active management component of the actively managed fund's five-year annualized return.

For example, assume that the benchmark fund has a five-year annualized return of 20 percent and the actively managed fund has a five-year annualized return of 22 percent. Subtracting the benchmark's five-year annualized return from the actively managed fund's five-year annualized return leaves us with a balance of 2 percent. Dividing the 2 percent balance by the actively managed fund's five-year annualized return 22 percent gives us a result of 11 percent, which equals the active management component's contribution to the actively managed fund's five-year annualized return.

The final step in computing the actively managed fund's Active Management Value Ratio™ is to compare the active component of the actively managed fund's annual expense fee to the active management component's contribution to the actively managed fund's five-year annualized return. In our example, a plan participant would have to question the value of investing in the actively managed fund, as the 80 percent active component of the fund's annual fees is only contributing 11 percent to the actively managed fund's five-year annualized return.

Put another way, a plan participant could have achieved basically the same five-year annualized return for twenty percent of the cost of the actively managed fund. With the increase in so-called "closet indexers," fund managers showing a tendency to avoid significant deviations from applicable benchmark indexes in order to avoid losing customers, the Active Management Value Ratio™ calculation becomes even more valuable to plan participants.

Both the correlation of returns data and the Active Management Value Ratio™ provide valuable information that plan participants can easily use to better protect their financial security. And yet plan participants are not provided with this information or other helpful information.

While it is true that neither ERISA nor the Department of Labor specifically requires that such information be provided to plan participants, it can be argued that the failure to provide such information is inconsistent with ERISA's requirement that plan participants be provided with "sufficient information to make an informed decision" with regard to their retirement accounts. The current Department of Labor and ERISA requirement that only historical return and risk information has to be provided to plan participants relegates plan participants to the pre-MPT standards and ignores the establishment of MPT's principles as the standards of prudence by both the Department of Labor and the courts.

Since ERISA requires that plan fiduciaries must always put the interests of the plan participants and their beneficiaries first, why are plan participants not provided with such important information such as correlation of returns and the Active Management Value Ratio™? Read on.

Chapter Seven

Countering Conflicts of Interest

An investment in knowledge pays the best interest.
Benjamin Franklin

Stockbroker's job is not to make money for you.
Their job is to make money from you.
Charles Ellis

ERISA plan sponsors are required to provide plan participants with certain information regarding both the plan and the plan's investment alternatives. More specifically, ERISA requires that plan sponsors are required to provide plan participants with "sufficient information to make an informed decision" with regard to their retirement accounts.

So why do plan participants often fail to receive helpful information such as correlation of returns data and the Active Management Value Ratio™? In many cases the failure can be traced to a conflict of interests between the plan providers, the plan sponsors and the plan participants.

The situation is often compounded by so-called investment education programs that are, at best, a marketing presentation and, at worst, a presentation that misrepresents the value and proper means of diversification. These bogus investment education presentations often result in what may be referred to as "pseudo" diversification, leaving a plan participant with little or no downside protection against downturns in the market.

What are the chances that plan providers will disclose problems with and questionable aspects of the investments that they recommended to the plan sponsor? And yet, if ERISA's "sufficient information" requirement is to be honored, a valid argument can be made that plan participants have a right to, as well as a need for, such information in order to effectively manage their retirement accounts.

Information on the correlation of returns between the investment alternatives available under a plan would be very beneficial in helping plan participants create an effectively diversified portfolio in order to avoid large investment losses. However, if plan providers provide such information to the plan and the plan participants, it might expose the fact that many of the investment alternatives within the plan have a high correlation of returns, effectively reducing the viable investment alternatives that the plan participants have to choose from to create an effectively diversified investment portfolio.

The Active Management Value Ratio™ is a relatively new analytical tool. Given the newness of the Active Management Value Ratio™, it is understandable why plan providers have not provided plans and plan participants with Active Management Value Ratio™ ratings. However, there are other means of analyzing investments on a cost-benefit analysis. Yet, I have never seen an instance in which a plan provider has provided a plan or plan participants with any meaningful form of a cost-benefit analysis for the investment alternatives that the plan provider has recommended to a plan.

Studies have consistently shown that actively managed mutual funds underperform similar passively managed, or index, funds. For example

- A miniscule 4 percent of [mutual] funds produce market-beating, after-tax results with a scant 0.6 percent (annual) margin of gain. The 96 percent of funds that fail to meet or beat the Vanguard 500 Index fund lose by a wealth-destroying margin of 4.8 percent per annum.[1]

- At the end of 2007, index funds accounted for only slightly more than 5 percent of the mutual funds assets, leaving about 95 percent of assets in the hands of wealth-destroying active managers. In a rational world, the percentages would be reversed.[2]

- The historical record shows that on a cumulative basis, over three-quarters of professionally managed mutual funds underperform the S&P 500 stock market index…over the very long term, 85 percent of active managers fall short of the market….In fact, given the cost of active management – fees, commissions, market impact of big transactions, and so forth – 85 percent of investment managers have and will continue over the long term to underperform the overall market.[3]

- Bear markets should generally favor active managers. In the two true bear markets over the last decade, most active managers failed to beat their benchmarks.[4]

- The only consistent data point we have observed over the five year horizon is that a majority of active equity and bond managers in most categories lag comparable benchmark indices.[45]

The last comment is from Standard and Poor's (S&P) annual study comparing the performance of actively managed funds to a comparable S&P index. The study, commonly referred to as the "SPIVA Scorecard," has consistently shown that the indices outperform the actively managed funds.

For the period ending on December 31, 2011, the SPIVA Scorecard showed the indices outperforming 84.07 percent of all actively managed funds over a one- year period; outperforming 56.53 percent of all actively managed funds over a three-year period; and outperforming 61.88 percent of all actively-managed funds over a five-year period.[6] Other annual SPIVA studies show similar results.

It would clearly not be in a plan provider's best interests to provide a plan or plan participants with a report that shows that they could achieve similar, if not better, results at a significantly lower price by choosing index mutual funds. And yet, the failure to disclose such information is inconsistent with ERISA's goal of protecting plan participants and their beneficiaries.

A plan fiduciary choosing actively managed investment alternatives with both poor performance records and significantly higher annual expenses relative to index funds could hardly be said to be in compliance with the fiduciary duty of prudence. Once again, the best advice for plan participants is to maintain a healthy dose of skepticism and to trust, but verify.

Chapter Eight

Mutual Funds

We all know that active management fees are high. Poor performance does not come cheap. You have to pay dearly for it.
Rex Sinquefield

Mutual funds are the most common form of investment alternatives in retirement plans, especially 401(k) and 457(b) plans. A mutual fund can be thought of as a company that pools money from various investors that have common investment goals. The company creates an investment portfolio for the fund by investing in various types of investments that are consistent with their investors' goals. Each share, or unit, of the fund represents an investor's ownership rights and interests in the fund.

Mutual funds offer various advantages to investors, including

- Simplified Investing – a wide variety of funds to choose from and greater liquidity in redeeming and/or selling shares
- Reduced costs
- Professional management
- Diversification

There are, however, potential disadvantages to mutual funds that need to be considered, including

- The lack of customization for an investor's personal circumstances and/or financial needs
- Increased risk exposure due to the volatility of the stock market
- Potentially higher costs due to differences in fees and other costs.

Types of Mutual Funds

The two most common types of mutual funds are open-end and closed-end mutual funds. As the name implies, open-end mutual funds offer new shares to the public on an ongoing basis and are redeemed by the fund that issued the shares. Closed-end funds are more like stocks in that the fund is only authorized to offer a fixed number of shares, and investors wishing to buy or sell closed-end fund shares must do so in the open market.

Exchange-traded funds (ETFs) are a growing trend in investing. ETFs have largely been passively managed funds that represent investments in a particular sector of the stock market, e.g., stock market indices, industries, countries. There is currently a push to offer investors actively managed ETFs as well, although that development is still a work in progress.

Unit investment trusts (UITs) are investment funds that often invest in one type of investment, such as real estate and natural resources. UITs have a fixed term. Once the UIT's investment portfolio has been created, there is usually no further management of the fund. Once the IUT's fixed term is over, the fund's assets are sold and the proceeds divided among the UIT's investors.

Funds are also classified in terms of being passively managed or actively managed. Passively managed funds are often referred to as index funds, as they often invest in stock market indices or other forms of investment indices. Passively managed funds are just that, passively managed, save for perhaps an occasional rebalancing to ensure that the fund does replicate the applicable index.

Actively managed funds are actively managed in accordance with the fund's goals and the terms of the fund's rules and guidelines. The greater flexibility afforded to actively managed funds to respond to market inefficiencies and changes in the economy purportedly provides investors with a better opportunity to achieve greater returns than those of passive index funds.

Mutual Fund Fees and Costs
A decided drawback to mutual funds can be the various fees and other costs associated with a fund. A sample of the various fees includes

- Purchase Sales Charge (Front-End Load)
- Deferred Sales Charge (Back-End Load)
- Annual Management Fee

- 12b-1 Marketing/Distribution Fee
- Redemption Fee
- Annual Fund Operating Fees

In addition to the fees set out above, mutual fund investors also have to deal with various "hidden" fees and costs, such as brokerage transaction fees, custodian fees, directors' fees, legal fees and sales fees/commissions.

Mutual funds are offered to investors in various forms, or share classes. Mutual fund share classes are generally based on the load structure that the fund uses. Some of the most common share classes are

- No-load shares– the fund charges no front-end (purchase) or back-end (redemption) fees on its funds. The fund may charge an annual 12b-1, or marketing, fee.

- Class A shares – the fund charges a one-time front-end load on its funds, with discounts on the load usually being offered by the fund based on the amount being invested. The fund may charge an annual 12b-1, or marketing, fee.

- Class B shares – the fund charges a back-end load fee rather than a front-end load, but only if the investor redeems their shares prior to expiration of the redemption period. Many funds offering Class B shares use redemption schedules that reduce the amount of the back-end load annually over the redemption period.

  Many mutual fund companies offer a conversion feature that allows investors to convert Class B shares into Class A shares after a certain period of time. The conversion feature can help investors avoid the generally higher annual 12b-1 fees of Class B shares.

- Class C shares – the fund charges an annual 12b-1 fee that is usually higher than the 12b-1 fees charged by Class A and Class B shares. The annual 1 percent fee typically charged on Class C shares is equivalent to the annual management fee usually charged by registered investment advisers under the Investment Advisers Act of 1940. Class C shares are often used by stockbrokers as a means of collecting an annual advisory fee without registering as an investment adviser, as required by law.

Class C shares may also charge a one-time front-end load charge.

- Institutional shares – these are shares often offered to institutional clients, including retirement plans, where the front-end load is either significantly reduced from the load charged by retail Class A shares or waived altogether.

Retirement plan participants will hopefully have knowledgeable plan sponsors and will only have to deal with either no-load mutual funds, such as low cost index funds, and/or institutional shares where the front-end load is waived. Class C shares should never be in a retirement plan due to their costs. I have seen retirement plans offering Class A shares as an investment alternative. I have never seen a retirement plan offering Class B shares.

Once again, the optimal situation would be a retirement plan that offers either no-load mutual funds, such as low cost index funds, and/or institutional shares with any front-end load waived. If a retirement plan does not offer either of these classes of mutual fund shares, plan participants should talk to their plan sponsor, stress the prudence of such investment alternatives, and request that such investment alternatives be offered within their plan.

Chapter Nine

Variable Annuities – The Most Over-hyped, Most Oversold and Least Understood Investment Product in America

Treat [elderly annuity customers] like they're blind 12-year olds…
It's about putting a pitchfork in their chest.
Ellen Schultz and Jeff D, Opdyke,
"At Annuity University…Pitch to Seniors,"
The Wall Street Journal, July 2, 2002

Information about variable annuity purchases reveals that they
do not appear to be based on educated decisions.
Cerulli Associates

Variable annuities are one of the most over-hyped, most oversold, and least understood investment products. A popular industry saying is that "annuities are sold, not bought." Variable annuity salesmen use various sales pitches to convince investors to purchase a variable annuity. However, as is often the case, what is unsaid is often as important, if not more important, than what is said. This information gap can have serious financial consequences for plan participants.

Basic Structure of Annuities

Before analyzing some of the popular sales pitches used by variable annuity salesmen, it is important to understand the basic structure of a variable annuity. A variable annuity can be described as an insurance contract wrapped around mutual fund-like subaccounts. The presence of the insurance "wrapper" allows the variable annuity to provide tax-deferred growth.

Variable annuities typically charge two primary fees, an annual insurance fee and an annual subaccount management fee. The insurance fee usually consists of a mortality and expense (M&E) charge, usually in the range of 1.25-1.4 percent of the accumulated value of the variable annuity, and an administrative fee, usually in the range of 0.15-0.20 percent of the accumulated value of the variable annuity.

The M&E charge covers the guaranteed death benefit (GDB), which ensures that in the event that the owner of the variable annuity dies before annuitizing the variable annuity, their heirs will receive no less than the amount that the owner had invested in the variable annuity. The M&E charge also covers commission payments and general overhead expenses. The administrative fee covers various administrative expenses.

The subaccount management fee is charged for the professional management of the subaccount, much like the annual management fee charged by mutual funds. Subaccount management fees can vary depending on the type of account, with management fees typically falling within the 0.80-1.00 percent range.

The total annual fee charged on most variable annuities is approximately 2 percent of the overall value of the variable annuity. When compared to an average annual management fee of 1 percent for actively managed mutual funds, 0.45 percent for passively managed mutual funds, and the typically low annual fees for exchange traded funds (ETFs), it is easy to see why the high fees and expenses associated with variable annuities are criticized, especially when their drag on long term performance is factored in.

Annuity Sales Pitches

So why do people continue to invest in variable annuities? Remember, annuities are sold, not bought. An analysis of some of the sales pitches used by variable annuity salesmen, in terms of what is said and what is unsaid, may prove helpful.

What's said: "Variable annuities offer tax deferred growth."

What's unsaid: 401(k), 403(b) and 457(b) plans, as well as individual retirement accounts (IRAs), already offer tax deferred growth without the high fees and expenses associated with variable annuities. Even investors in stocks, mutual funds, and ETFs can achieve virtual tax-deferred growth as long as they do not actively trade their accounts and they choose investments with low turnover rates (e.g., passively managed funds such as index funds and most ETFs) and low income pay-outs.

The value of the tax-deferred growth offered by variable annuities is reduced by the impact of the high fees and expenses associated with variable annuities. As previously mentioned, a study by the Department of Labor estimated that over a twenty year period, each additional 1 percent in fees reduces an investor's end return by 17 percent.[1]

Various studies have been done comparing the cost of investing in variable annuities to the cost of investing in mutual funds. These studies have generally concluded that in most cases it takes a minimum of 15-20 years, in some cases over forty years, for the owner of a variable annuity to break-even from the fees and expenses of variable annuities. In some cases, the owner of the variable annuity may never break-even.[2]

An article by Dr. William Reichenstein of Baylor University provides an excellent in-depth analysis of the effects of fees on the overall return realized by variable annuity and mutual fund investors. Among Reichenstein's findings: (1) that costs have a significant effect on the overall effectiveness of an investment, (2) that low cost mutual funds and low cost annuities are the most effective investments for investors, and (3) that the typical variable annuity, with a fee of 2 percent or more and an annual contract fee of $20-$30, is the least effective investment for investors.[3]

The value of the tax-deferred growth offered by variable annuities is also reduced by the tax aspects of a variable annuity, as compared to a mutual fund. Tax-deferred does not mean tax-free. Sooner or later, the variable annuity owner or their beneficiaries will have to pay income tax on the capital appreciation within the variable annuity.

Mutual fund owners can often use the capital gains tax rates to reduce the taxes on their mutual funds. Variable annuity owners cannot use the capital gains tax rate, as disbursements from variable annuities are taxed as ordinary income, which usually results in more tax liability and less money for the variable annuity owner or their beneficiaries.

What's said: "You don't pay sales charges when you purchase a variable annuity, so all of your money goes to work for you, unlike mutual funds that charge front-end sales charges, and stocks and ETFs, which require an investor to pay brokerage commissions."

What's Unsaid: There are excellent no-load mutual funds that perform as well as, and often better than, variable annuity subaccounts. These no-load mutual funds usually charge annual management fees far less that those charged for variable annuity subaccounts, especially passively managed mutual funds such as index funds. Investors purchasing stocks and ETFs can use discount brokers to greatly reduce the amount of any brokerage commissions.

The statement that variable annuity owners pay no sales charges, while technically correct, can be somewhat misleading. Variable annuity salesmen do receive a commission for each variable annuity they sell, such commission usually being in the range of 6-7 percent of the total amount invested in the variable annuity. While a purchaser of a variable annuity is not directly assessed a front-end sales charge or a brokerage commission, the variable annuity owner does reimburse the insurance company for the commission that was paid. The primary source of such reimbursement is through the variable annuity's various fees and charges, particularly the M&E charge.

To ensure that the cost of commissions paid is recovered, the insurance company typically imposes surrender charges on a variable annuity owner who tries to cash out of the variable annuity before the expiration of a certain period of time. The terms of these surrender charges vary, but a typical surrender charge schedule might provide for an initial surrender charge of 7 percent for withdrawals during the first year, decreasing 1 percent each year thereafter until the eighth year, when the surrender charges would end. There are some surrender charge schedules that charge a flat rate, such as 7 percent, over the entire surrender charge period.

One recent variable annuity innovation that has caused regulators a great deal of concern has been the so-called "bonus" annuities. These products have been marketed in such a way that the public may believe that they receive a free bonus, usually in the range of 3-4 percent of their investment, upon their purchase of the annuity. In truth, the insurance company sponsoring the bonus annuity may simply increase the term and/or the amount of the surrender charge to recover the "bonus." These bonus annuities continue to be the subject of much scrutiny due to their potential to mislead and deceive the public into thinking that they are receiving something that they really are not receiving.

Prospective annuity purchasers should always study the surrender charge schedule to minimize potential costs. Since surrender charge schedules often reflect the amount of commissions paid to the variable annuity salesman, an investor can compare the commission paid on a variable annuity (typically 6-7 percent) and the commission charged by front-end load mutual funds (typically 4-5 percent).

What's said: "Variable annuities offer a guaranteed death benefit (GDB) that ensures that the variable annuity owner's heirs will get no less than the amount of money that the variable annuity owner invested in the variable annuity.

What's unsaid: Most variable annuities discontinue the GDB once the variable annuity owner reaches a certain age. Furthermore, a variable annuity owner also generally loses the GDB if the owner elects to annuitize the variable annuity in order to receive the guaranteed lifetime income benefits.

The value of the GDB itself is questionable. Variable annuities are intended to be long term investments. Given the long term historical performance of the stock market, it is highly unlikely that a variable annuity owner will need to use the GDB since, over the long-term, the accumulated value of the variable annuity will probably exceed the amount of the GDB.

In his article, Dr. Reichenstein refers to studies that have estimated that the GDB is worth approximately 0.087 percent or less, although insurance companies currently impose M&E charges in the range to 1.25-1.4 percent to cover their GDB liability.[4]

Another interesting fact about the M&E charge is that while the GDB in most variable annuities only insures the variable annuity owner's investment in the variable annuity, the principal, the M&E charge is calculated based upon the accumulated value of the of the variable annuity, which includes both the principal and all capital appreciation within the annuity. This would seem to be clearly inequitable to the variable annuity owner who is forced to pay a higher amount of M&E charges as the value of the variable annuity increases, with no corresponding increase in the insurance company's obligation to the variable annuity owner.

For an additional fee, some insurance companies do offer a benefit that steps-up the amount of the GDB to the overall value of the variable annuity on certain anniversary dates. Given the unlikely need to use the GDB at all, the value of yet another layer of cost is equally questionable.

What's said: "Variable annuities can provide a lifetime stream of income, guaranteeing that you'll never run out of money to live on.

What's unsaid: To get the lifetime stream of income, the variable annuity owner generally has to annuitize the variable annuity. Upon annuitization, the variable annuity owner will receive a monthly payment, with the amount of the payment being based upon the owner's age and the settlement option that was chosen. The decision to annuitize should only be made after consideration of all of the consequences of such a decision.

Upon annuitization, the variable annuity owner gives up control of the annuity's assets. Even more important, depending on the settlement alternatives offered by the insurance company and the settlement option chosen by the variable annuity owner, once the variable annuity is annuitized the insurance company, not the owner's heirs, will receive any money left in the annuity when the owner dies.

Some variable annuities may require the owner of a variable annuity to annuitize their annuity upon reaching a certain age. Prospective variable annuity purchasers should always check the terms of a variable annuity being considered to see if the annuity contains such forced annuitization language, as it could frustrate an investor's estate plans.

Annuitization is, in essence, a gamble. The insurance company is hoping that the variable annuity owner dies before depleting all of the assets in the annuity, in which case the insurance company may receive the balance remaining in the annuity. The annuity owner, on the other hand, is gambling that they will live long enough to deplete the assets in their annuity.

What's said: "You can roll money over from your 401(k) or other retirement account into an IRA and then purchase a variable annuity for such account. You'll continue to receive tax deferred growth of your money and you'll get the safety of the guaranteed death benefit."

What's unsaid: Qualified plans and IRAs already offer tax deferred growth. Consequently, purchasing a variable annuity within an IRA simply adds the high fees and expenses of the variable annuity without providing the investor with any meaningful additional benefits.

Many people work hard during their lifetime to accumulate funds not only for their retirement, but also to create an estate to leave to their heirs. Annuitization can result in an insurance company, not one's heirs, inheriting the results of one's hard work.

While IRA owners must begin to take disbursements from an IRA once they reach a certain age, the balance remaining in the IRA at the owner's death passes to their designated beneficiaries. There are also various ways to minimize the amount of the required disbursements from an IRA so that the IRA assets can benefit one's children, grandchildren and beyond.

Placing a variable annuity within an IRA may result in a forced annuitization because of the required disbursements from an IRA at age 70½ or because of language in the variable annuity requiring annuitization at a certain age or upon the occurrence of some event. Such a forced annuitization may result in consequences unintended, and undesired, by the IRA owner, including the owner's heirs' loss of their inheritance.

The questionable value of the GDB has already been discussed. The GDB is simply insurance. An investor who needs insurance and the GDB it provides should buy insurance, but through more cost effective alternatives, such as term insurance.

What's said: "You'll have access to your money at all times since variable annuities typically allow an owner to withdraw up to 10 percent from their annuity annually, after the first year, without any penalty."

What's unsaid: The insurance company's decision to waive any penalties does not change the fact that all withdrawals from a variable annuity result in tax consequences. Withdrawal of gains from variable annuities are taxed as ordinary income. Variable annuity owners cannot use the capital gains tax rates to reduce their tax liability. In addition, withdrawals made by an owner prior to reaching the age of 59½ are generally subject to a penalty tax equal to 10 percent of the amount withdrawn.[5]

Many variable annuities allow an owner to withdraw more than 10 percent in a limited number of circumstances. In the event that unanticipated circumstances arise during the period that the variable annuity's surrender charges are applicable, and such circumstances are not among those specified for allowing withdrawals beyond the insurance company's annual allowance, the variable annuity owner may have to pay the applicable surrender charges in addition to the ordinary income and penalty taxes.

What's said: "If you're ever dissatisfied with the performance of your variable annuity, you can switch to another variable annuity without paying any taxes."

What's unsaid: Tax-free annuity exchanges, known as "1035 exchanges," present a number of issues. Both the Financial Industry Regulatory Association (FINRA) and the SEC have made questionable variable annuity sales tactics, including 1035 exchanges, a priority.

There are reports that 1035 exchanges account for a significant portion of annual variable annuity sales.[6] Brokers and advisors like 1035 exchanges since they result in new commissions for the broker or the advisor. Variable annuity owners contemplating such an exchange should note that any 1035 exchange made while the existing variable annuity is subject to surrender charges will result in the owner having to pay such surrender charges.

In addition, if the new variable annuity imposes surrender charges, those surrender charges begin anew. Consequently, prior to making a 1035 exchange, a variable annuity owner whose annuity is free of surrender charges should carefully consider the costs and the limitations that new surrender charges may create.

Generally speaking, a variable annuity owner should only consider making a 1035 exchange if (1) the existing annuity is not subject to any surrender charges, and (2) the existing variable annuity is being exchanged for a new annuity that has low or no surrender charges and lower fees and expenses than the existing variable annuity. Owners of variable annuities issues prior to 1982 should consult with a tax expert prior to making a 1035 exchange due to the special tax issues associated with such annuities.

What's said: "If you're ever dissatisfied with the performance of a subaccount in your variable annuity, you can switch to another subaccount without having to pay sales loads or taxes."

What's unsaid: While a mutual fund investor can choose from the entire universe of mutual funds, the variable annuity owner is limited to those subaccounts that are offered within the variable annuity.

Some variable annuities offer over twenty subaccounts, while others may offer ten or less. In some cases, the insurance company sponsoring the variable annuity may limit all, or a majority, of the available subaccounts to their proprietary products. Quite often, these proprietary products have less than stellar performance records. It should also be noted that some variable annuities do impose a fee, usually in the range of $20-25 per switch, if the variable annuity owner exceeds a certain number of subaccount switches in a year.

What's said: "The tax deferred growth offered by a variable annuity will allow you to pass more money on to your heirs."

What's unsaid: Variable annuities are terrible estate planning tools. If the variable annuity is ever annuitized, the variable annuity owner loses control of the annuity's assets and, depending on the settlement alternatives offered and chosen, the insurance company, not the owner's heirs, may get any money remaining in the annuity when the owner dies.

If the variable annuity owner never annuitizes the annuity, then their heirs do receive the greater of the owner's actual investment in the variable annuities or the value of the variable annuity at the owner's death. The beneficiaries of a variable annuity must pay income tax on the portion of the proceeds that represent the capital appreciation within the annuity. Such proceeds are taxed as ordinary income instead of capital gains, generally resulting in higher taxes and significantly less money for the owner's beneficiaries.

Heirs receiving mutual funds, stocks, and ETFs as their inheritance pay no taxes due to the step-up in basis these investment products receive upon an owner's death. The value of this estate planning benefit cannot be overstated, as it allows heirs to avoid the taxes associated with variable annuities and allows the owner to pass more of the estate to their heirs

Equity Indexed Annuities

Much has been written about the advantages of investing in index mutual funds. Index mutual funds became even more popular during the bull market of the late 80's and the 90's, as indexes regularly reported annual double-digit gains. The annuity industry quickly responded by offering index-based annuities, commonly known as equity indexed annuities. While equity indexed annuities are technically fixed, rather than variable, annuities, they merit discussion due to the fact that they are usually tied to an equity market index.

Some might say that the marketing of equity indexed annuities can mislead the public due to the severe restrictions placed on the indexed annuity owner's ability to fully participate in an index's gain. Most equity-indexed annuities limit, or "cap," the owner's annual gain to an arbitrary percentage regardless of the index's actual gain. The owner's ability to participate in the index's gain is further restricted by the imposition of a "participation rate," typically in the range of 70-80 percent.

For example, if an investor owned an equity indexed annuity that capped the annuity owner's annual gain at 10 percent, with a participation rate of 70 percent, the most that the annuity owner could earn for that year would be 7 percent (10 percent x .70), even if the index actually gained 30 percent that year.

Some equity-indexed annuities do offer downside protection by guaranteeing a minimum annual return, usually related to prevailing interest rates. Nevertheless, when an investor in an index based product is limited to a gain of 7 percent when the index itself shows a much larger gain, it is easy to understand why some investors may question the inherent value and fairness of the product.

Riders

Most annuities offer the owner a variety of additional benefits in exchange for additional fees. These benefits are offered in the form of additional contract provisions, or "riders." The number of potential riders is too large to allow a complete discussion here. The prospective investor should analyze each rider offered to determine the true value of the benefit, if any, being offered and the effect of the additional fees.

One rider currently being offered is called an "enhanced death benefit" (EDB). The lack of a stepped-up basis for variable annuities is often an impediment to their purchase. In an effort to counter this disadvantage, the EDB pays an additional amount of money to the heirs in an attempt to mitigate the effect of the ordinary income tax that they must pay. The value of the EDB is very questionable due to the way that it is calculated and the fact that the EDB itself is also taxable. More often than not, the variable annuity owner will determine that the benefit offered by the rider simply does not justify its added cost.

Decisions

Do variable annuities ever make sense? Prospective annuity purchaser should remember Dr. Reichenstein's findings that the typical variable annuity sold by variable annuity salesmen, with annual fees and expenses of approximately 2 percent and an annual contract fee, is always a poor investment choice.[7] Investors should also look at the number and type of subaccounts offered within the variable annuity, the performance record of each subaccount, and the annual management fee charged by the subaccounts.

What alternatives are available to investors who already own a variable annuity and are either dissatisfied with the performance of their annuity or question whether an annuity was a suitable investment for them? The question of suitability depends on various factors such as the investor's age, investment objectives, financial needs, risk tolerance level, income, and need for liquidity. Suitability determinations are best handled by a truly objective source such as an attorney or a fee-only financial planner who has a background in annuities or securities compliance.

If a determination is made that the annuity was an unsuitable investment for the investor, the investor may choose to contact the broker and brokerage firm that sold them the annuity, as well as the insurance company that sponsors the annuity, and request that the variable annuity contract be rescinded and that their original investment be refunded in full. Given the current investigations by regulatory agencies such as FINRA and the Securities and Exchange Commission into questionable annuity sales practices, the sanctions that have already been assessed in some cases, and pending legal actions involving the sale of annuities, investors with suitability questions should consider seeking a professional evaluation and objective advice regarding their situation to ensure that they are not exposing themselves to unnecessary financial losses due to unsuitable investments.

Variable annuity owners whose annuity was suitable, but who are dissatisfied with the costs and/or the performance of their annuity should consider exchanging their annuity for an annuity with lower costs, low or no surrender charges, and/or a better performance record once the surrender charge period on their present annuity expires. Annuity exchanges involving annuities that are still subject to surrender charges are generally discouraged due to the loss that would be created in having to pay the surrender charges.

Another example of the variable annuity industry's seeming indifference to the best interests of the client can be seen in stories and reports prepared or sponsored by the industry comparing investments in annuities to investments in mutual funds. Close analysis of such stories and reports usually reveal that the opinions are based on assumptions heavily favoring the annuities, such as assuming that investors will only invest in mutual funds with high fees and that the fund and/or the investor will generate substantial capital gains by heavily trading the fund/account. Without such assumptions, the chances that the variable annuity will outperform the mutual fund are greatly reduced. The danger is that inexperienced investors, however, may not be able to detect such biases.

Rarely, if ever, will you find an industry-prepared or industry-sponsored analysis comparing an investment in a variable annuity to an investment in a low cost mutual fund, particularly an index fund. The low annual fees and passive management associated with index funds virtually guarantee that the variable annuity will always lose out in such comparisons. Long-term owners of stocks and ETFs could also outperform variable annuities as well since the stocks and ETFs would not be burdened by high annual fees and annual capital gains.

Bottom line – variable annuities, just say no.

Chapter Ten

Target-date Funds

*Shockingly, the basic premise upon which these billions
[of dollars in target-date funds] are invested is flawed.*
Rob Arnott

The Department of Labor has designated certain types of investments as "qualified default investment alternatives" (QDIAs) for retirement plans.[1] Generally speaking, as long as a plan sponsor satisfies all applicable prudence requirements, the plan sponsor can use QDIAs to potentially reduce their personal liability exposure. Plan fiduciaries that choose to use QDIAs still remain liable for their choice of QDIAs and their duty to monitor such QDIAs to ensure their ongoing suitability.

Target-date funds are a popular choice within retirement plans, both as QDIAs and as a general investment alternative. Target-date funds basically create an asset allocation mix based upon the "target-date" for the fund, using both equity-based investments and fixed income investments. The target-date often corresponds to the investor's projected year of retirement.

Target-date funds are primarily passively managed investments. The fund establishes a timetable for when the fund's asset allocation will be adjusted. The timetable, referred to as the fund's "glide path," usually involves reducing the fund's equity allocation and increasing the fund's fixed income allocation as the target date gets closer. By gradually reducing the fund's equity allocation over time, the fund supposedly reduces the fund's overall risk in accordance with the investors' approaching need for their funds at the fund's target date.

While target-date funds appear appealing on their face, plan participants and plan sponsors need to understand that not all target-date funds are managed the same way and that even target-date funds have definite risks and disadvantages. The risks inherent in a target-fund involve the fund's asset allocation mix, the fund's management philosophy, and the fund's fees and costs.

Target-date funds can vary greatly with regard to the riskiness of the portfolio they choose to create. Funds may vary with regard to the riskiness of the assets chosen and/or with regard to the allocation percentages within the fund's portfolio. An investor in a target-date fund has no control over the investments within the fund or the allocation between equity investments and fixed-income investments.

With target-date funds, changes in a fund's allocation mix are generally done strictly according to the fund's timetable. This inflexible and mechanical approach to asset allocation can, and often does, result in unnecessary risk exposure for the fund's investors and poor performance for the fund.

Another example of the potential risks resulting from a target-date fund's management philosophy involves whether a fund adopts a "to" or "through" management approach. The term "to or through" refers to whether the fund continues to re-allocate the fund's assets beyond, or through, the fund's target-date. Target-date funds that adopt a "through" approach often justify their approach on a perceived need for an investor's continuing exposure to equity-based investments to ensure that the investors do not outlive their assets, even though the "through" exposure may carry a higher degree of risk than the investor needs or can afford.

Just as with any investment, the impact of fees cannot be ignored. Fees reduce an investor's returns. In the case of target-date funds, the average annual fee is generally in line with actively managed mutual funds. Given the fact that target-date funds usually employ a passive management approach and have a generally poor performance record, the fees charged by target-date funds are difficult to defend.

The mechanical, passive management approach used by most target-date funds often results in greater volatility for the fund, as well as increased and unnecessary risk exposure for fund investors. Critics of target-date funds have argued that the funds need to improve their risk management skills by better integrating active management within the fund's glide path. In the words of one critic,

The volatility (and correlation) level of the assets in the portfolio at a specific point in time are also an integral part of the equation....Glide path is the most important part of a target-date fund, yet conventional approaches allocate little time to managing it.[2]

In summary, a target-date fund is essentially an index fund, passively managed in strict accordance with a pre-set schedule for re-allocating the fund's assets. This mechanical approach generally results in little or no risk management protection for investors, often resulting in unnecessary financial losses for investors. And yet the Department of Labor has approved target-date funds as a default investment product for plan participants. Surely there has to be better, more effective investment alternatives for plan participants.

Chapter Eleven

Risk Management – The Secret to Successful Investing

Protect the downside and the upside will take care of itself.
Donald Trump

Investment planning is about structuring exposure to risk factors.
Eugene Fama, Jr.

Two well-known sayings on Wall Street are "amateurs focus on returns, professionals focus on risk," and "don't tell me how much money you made, tell how much you were able to keep." In his seminal book, "Winning the Loser's Game," Charles Ellis states that risk management is the key to investment success.[1] And yet most investment advertisements focus entirely on the investment's returns and/or their returns relative to their competitors, with no mention whatsoever of their investment's level of risk.

Truth be told, it simply is not that difficult to make money in a bull, or upward trending, market. History has shown that approximately 75 percent of stocks follow the overall trend of the stock market. This fact leads to the warning regarding evaluating stock brokers and investment advisers, the warning of "don't confuse brains with a bull market." Likewise, it is not that difficult to suffer significant losses in a bear, or downward trending, market.

Proper risk management is not about catching every up or avoiding every down in the stock market. Proper risk management is about minimizing the potential of large losses in one's investment portfolio.

Many investors fail to truly understand the impact of investment losses. An example I often use to illustrate the impact of investment losses is to ask the audience where an investor stands if the investor suffers a 50 percent loss in one year, followed by a 50 percent gain the following year. Most people will say that the investor has broken even since the amount of the loss and gain are the same.

In fact, the investor still has a 25 percent loss in their portfolio since the 50 percent gain is applied to a much lower portfolio balance due to the initial 50 percent loss. An investor with a beginning balance of $10,000 only has a balance of $5,000 after a 50 percent loss. A 50 percent gain the next year leaves an investor with a balance of only $7,500 in their account, $2,500, or 25 percent, less than their account's original balance.

The impact of investment losses can be seen even more dramatically as a result of various studies comparing the benefits of being invested on the "best" days of the stock market to the benefits of avoiding the "worst" days of the stock market. The studies consistently show that the benefits of avoiding the "worst" days of the stock market far outweigh the benefits of being invested on the "best" days of the stock market.

Professor Javier Estrada of the IESE Business School studied the impact of missing the best and the worst days on the Dow Jones Industrial Average Index (DJIA). Professor Estrada found that over the period 1900-2006, missing the best 10, 20 and 100 days on the DJIA would have reduced an investor's terminal wealth by 65 percent, 83.2 percent and 99.7 percent respectively. Conversely, avoiding the 10, 20 and 100 worst days on the DJIA over the same time period would have increased an investor's terminal wealth by 206 percent, 531.5 percent and 43,396.8 percent respectively.[2]

Professor Estrada also performed a similar best days/worst days analysis on the DJIA for the period 1990-2006, finding that missing the best 10, 20 and 100 days on the DJIA would have reduced an investor's terminal wealth by 38 percent, 56.8 percent and 93.8 percent respectively. Conversely, avoiding the worst 10, 20 and 100 days on the DJIA over the same period would have improved an investor's terminal wealth by 70.1 percent, 140.6 percent and 1,619.1 percent respectively.[3]

The numbers support the potential advantages of implementing an effective risk management program to avoid significant market losses, especially when intermediate or long-term market and/or economic indicators indicate the possibility of a secular bear market.

The importance of risk management cannot be overemphasized. Fortunately for investors, an effective risk management program can be as simple as a well-designed asset allocation plan that results in an effectively diversified investment portfolio.

Chapter Twelve

Asset Allocation

Even if you're on the right track, you'll get run over if you just sit there.
Will Rogers

The best way to manage something is to take
advantage of its natural tendencies.
Lao Tzu

Asset allocation refers to investing in a mix of different types of investments, the "don't put all your eggs in one basket" approach to investing. Historically, the most common asset allocation for investment portfolios has centered around a 60 percent allocation to equity-based investments, such as stocks and equity-based mutual funds, and a 40 percent allocation to fixed income investments, such as bonds.

One of the subjects approved by the Department of Labor for investment education programs is asset allocation. The importance of asset allocation in a meaningful wealth management program is undeniable. Just as important, however, is understanding the true importance of effective asset allocation and separating the myth from reality.

There are those in the investment industry that are fond of claiming that asset allocation is the most important factor in successful investing. These people are quick to point to a famous study and to claim that the study showed that 93.6 percent of a portfolio's investment returns are due to asset allocation alone. The problem is that the study in question never made such a representation.

The study in question is commonly referred to as the BHB study, named after the three authors of the article.[1] The study analyzed a number of retirement plans in terms of the impact that their asset allocation decisions had on their plan's overall investment performance.

The study concluded that 93.6 percent of the <u>variability</u> of returns in a retirement plan could be attributed to the fund's asset allocation choices. Variability of returns is significantly different from actual returns. The BHB study did not, and did not claim to, analyze the role of asset allocation in producing investment returns.

If one considers the parameters of the study, the BHB study's findings actually are not surprising at all. The plans had three investment alternatives to choose from: stocks, bonds and cash. Stocks are historically more volatile than bonds and cash, and bonds are more volatile than cash. Therefore, what the BHB study basically said is that higher allocations to more volatile assets, such as stocks and bonds, increase the overall volatility of an investment portfolio. Perfectly understandable, but hardly surprising.

The investment industry has simply chosen to deliberately mislead investors to further the industry's own interests, to convince investors not to make changes in their portfolios so that the industry can receive ongoing annual fees from mutual fund companies and insurance companies at the investors' expense. Plan participants need to keep this in mind when service plan providers advise them against making changes in their portfolios and to consider potential conflicts of interest issues in such advice.

Done properly, asset allocation can help provide downside protection for a portfolio and reduce the potential for large investment losses. There are basically three schools of thought on asset allocation: static asset allocation, tactical asset allocation, and dynamic asset allocation.

Static asset allocation is a generally passive approach to asset allocation. Static asset allocation involves creating an asset allocation mix for a investment portfolio and consistently maintaining the same exact allocation by periodically rebalancing the portfolio to restore the original allocations. Static asset allocation is based in large part on the misinterpretation of the BHB study's findings as to the importance of asset allocation relative to portfolio returns.

Static asset allocation has been much maligned, both for its misplaced reliance on the BHB study and its tendency to leave investors exposed to unnecessary investment risk. Chinese philosopher Lao Tzu said that the easiest way to control something is to take advantage of its natural tendencies. Static asset allocation has been criticized for not recognizing and not taking advantage of the proven cyclical nature of the stock market.

Tactical asset allocation and dynamic asset allocation both advocate an active approach to asset allocation. Tactical asset allocation recommends asset allocation changes based upon market forecasts. Dynamic asset allocation involves making asset allocation changes in response to actual changes in economic and/or market conditions.

Both tactical and dynamic asset allocation have been criticized by some as examples of attempts to time the market, a practice which has been shown to be extremely difficult to perform successfully on a consistent basis. The classic definition of market timing has been a short-term investment strategy in which 100 percent of an investor's portfolio has been invested in either the stock market or cash. Since neither tactical asset allocation nor dynamic asset allocation advocate such an extreme asset allocation strategy, it can be argued that neither approach constitutes market timing.

If market timing is defined as reallocating a portfolio's assets so as to minimize the risk of large portfolio losses, then all three forms of asset allocation would be involved in market timing. Reallocating portfolio assets is simply a form of risk management, an often overlooked key to successful investing.

What many plan participants do not seem to understand is that avoiding large losses is much more important than trying to maximize returns. As previously noted, it takes a larger return to make up for an investment loss since you have less money with which to fund a recovery.

A plan participant who suffers an investment loss also suffers another loss, the opportunity to increase the value of their original portfolio since the plan participant has to use the market gain to simply restore their original portfolio balance. A plan participant will never get ahead if they have to spend all their time catching up.

Chapter Thirteen

Diversification

Diversification should be the corner stone of your investment program.
Sir John Templeton

To reduce risk it is necessary to avoid a portfolio whose
securities are all highly correlated with each other.
Harry Markowitz

Many people mistakenly believe that diversification and asset allocation are one and the same. However, that is not necessarily so. Diversification is, by definition, a form of asset allocation. Asset allocation, however, is not necessarily diversification, at least not effective diversification in terms of effective risk management. Understanding the difference is a key to preventing unnecessary investment losses.

As mentioned earlier, most plan-sponsored educational programs involve the presentation of various multi-colored pie charts representing model portfolios for the plan participants to consider, with the models recommending various allocations to different categories of mutual funds (e.g., large cap funds, small cap funds, mid cap funds, international funds, fixed-income funds). What plan participants are not told is that while all of the models represent forms of asset allocation, the models are often not effectively diversified due to the high correlation of returns between the equity-based investment alternatives within both the models and their retirement plan.

A simple example may help. Assume that an investment portfolio is equally divided among a large cap investment (the Standard & Poor's 500 Index), a small cap investment (the Russell 2000 Index), an international investment (the MSCI EAFE Index), and a fixed income investment (the Barclays U.S. Aggregate Bond Index). The portfolio is obviously allocated among four different asset categories. However, the portfolio is not effectively diversified in terms of risk management due to the high correlation of returns between the three equity-based investments.

The correlations of returns for the four investments over the five-year period 2007-2011 were as follows:

S&P 500 and Russell 2000	95 percent
S&P 500 and MSCI EAFE	92 percent
Russell 2000 and MSCI EAFE	84 percent
EAFE and Barclays Bond	20 percent
S&P 500 and Barclays Bond	10 percent
Russell 2000 and Barclays Bond	2 percent

The high correlation of returns between the equity-based investments effectively results in a portfolio that is composed of 75 percent equity investments and 25 percent fixed income investments, a portfolio that might not be suitable for many plan participants given the portfolio's high degree of potential risk. An analysis of recent rolling five-year periods of returns shows a similar pattern of high correlations of returns between the equity-based investments.

Plan participants can experiment with various online asset allocation programs and see for themselves the diversification issues discussed herein. Unless you choose the most conservative alternatives presented, most commercial and online asset allocation programs recommend portfolios that reflect the traditionally recommended 60 percent stock/40 percent bonds allocation.

What investors need to realize is that such a high allocation to equity-based investments may not be appropriate for their financial needs and/or their ability, or even need, to bear such investment risk, especially if the equity-based products show a high correlation of returns.

The challenge most plan participants will face in effectively diversifying their retirement account is the limited investment alternatives available within their plan that they can use to accomplish this goal. As plan participants who perform the correlation of returns calculations discover, most retirement plans are over-weighted with expensive, highly correlated, equity-based investment alternatives.

That is where the money is for plan providers, which is why the plan providers recommend such platforms and refuse to disclose correlation of returns information to both plan sponsors and plan participants. It is the reason why plan providers for all types of retirement plans, both ERISA and non-ERISA covered plans, should be required to disclose correlation of returns data for all investment alternatives in the plans that they recommend so that both plan sponsors and plan participants can truly evaluate the quality of the plan provider's recommendations.

This is one of the main reasons why ERISA needs to require that plan participants be provided with more than just historical risk and returns data. This is exactly why Markowitz introduced MPT and argued that correlation of returns must be considered in the portfolio construction process. Correlation of returns data is an absolute necessity if ERISA's "sufficient information to make informed decision" requirement is to be meaningful and if plan participants are to be given a real opportunity to effectively diversify their portfolios and protect their financial interests.

Chapter Fourteen

The "Absolute" Truth About Successful Investing

You can eat absolute returns; you can't eat relative returns.
Bob Reynolds

ERISA Section 404(c) gives ERISA retirement plans the opportunity to shift investment risk to the plan participants. Most plan participants, however, have neither the investment knowledge nor the investment experience to properly manage their retirement account. As mentioned previously, a recent study by the Securities and Exchange Commission concluded that most Americans are financially illiterate.[1]

Plan participants are faced with sorting through various investment material and various mutual fund advertisements claiming that they are the best investment choice, that they have outperformed all of their peers over the past "x" number of years and/or have been awarded "x" number of stars by Morningstar. Welcome to the world of meaningless investment ads.

First of all, such recommendations are based on past performance. Remember, as all investment advertisements are required to disclose, past performance is no guarantee of future results.

Second, such advertisements address relative performance and, therefore, can be highly misleading. A mutual fund that suffered a loss of 20 percent can truthfully claim that it outperformed its peers as long as its peers suffered larger losses over the same time period. Not many investors would gloat about paying high mutual fund fees to suffer a 20 percent loss in their portfolio.

The key for plan participants is to focus on consistently earning positive absolute returns. Absolute returns are the actual returns of an investment, without regard to any other mutual fund or mutual fund manager. The goal is to consistently earn positive returns so that an investor's retirement account benefits from compounding returns to maximize the plan participant's wealth.

Many plan participants confess that that simply choose their investments based upon the number of stars that Morningstar has assigned to a fund. The problem with such a selection system is that Morningstar's star system is based on past performance. Morningstar itself warns investors that their star system is not designed to be used to predict future performance.

Morningstar is an incredible resource. I constantly use Morningstar's resources and I recommend that plan participants use Morningstar in performing an Active Management Value Ratio™ analysis. However, studies have shown that Morningstar's star ratings are not necessarily persistent, even over relatively short periods of time,[2] yet another reason to focus on sources of consistent, absolute returns.

Unless an investor only invests in certificates of deposit, Treasury bills and other cash equivalents, odds are that an investor is going to suffer an investment loss along the way. Even an investor who only invests in cash equivalents is probably going to suffer a loss in the form of purchasing power due to inflation.

The key is for plan participants to invest wisely and to not be misled by all the investment advertisements touting their alleged accomplishments. By focusing on investments that have provided consistent absolute returns across different market environments, a plan participant can increase their chances for investment success.

Chapter Fifteen

Putting It All Together

*The essence of effective portfolio construction is the use
of a large number of poorly correlated assets.*
William Bernstein

Price is what you pay. Value is what you get.
Warren Buffett

So, how do we put all of this information together in a meaningful, yet relatively simple way so that plan participants and plan sponsors can better protect their interests?

Before we discuss the actual analytical process, it is important that plan participants request and receive all the disclosure material to which they are entitled under ERISA. The key documents were discussed in Chapter 5. While all of the documents may not be useful in the analytical process we recommend, plan participants should keep the documents in order to be aware of their plan's policies and procedures in order to protect their rights under the plan.

ERISA requires that, upon request, the plan must provide participants with a copy of the prospectuses for all of the investment alternatives available within the plan. Plan participants and sponsors should compare the information in the prospectuses with information available from commercial sources such as Morningstar and Lipper Analytical. While the information may vary due to the differences in the dates of such information, significant differences should be fully researched to determine which information is timelier and more reliable.

The first thing I do is to determine a fund's R-squared rating. R-squared is simply a fund's correlation coefficient squared. A fund's R-squared rating indicates to what extent a fund's performance is due to the performance of its relevant benchmark rather than the contribution of any active management provided by a fund.

Managers of actively managed mutual funds are becoming increasingly sensitive to their performance relative to benchmarks and index mutual funds, especially after the recent 2000-2002 and 2008 bear markets. A fund manager whose performance deviates too much from relative benchmarks and index funds face the potential loss of customers

As a result, more actively managed funds are showing performance numbers that closely track the performance numbers of benchmark index funds, thereby resulting in high R-squared ratings for many actively managed funds. Actively managed funds with high R-squared ratings are often referred to as "closet index" funds.

While there is no general consensus on the exact R-squared rating that qualifies an actively managed mutual as a closet index fund, most people agree that an R-squared rating of 90 or higher is probably sufficient. Some even deem a fund with an R-squared rating in the 80's to be a closet index fund.

Plan participants should eliminate a fund that qualifies as a closet index fund simply because such funds are usually not cost efficient. Actively managed funds generally impose annual expense fees that are significantly higher than index funds. Every additional increment of cost reduces an investor's end return. A fund's designation as a closet index fund indicates that an investor could usually earn similar, if not better, results with less cost by choosing a similar index fund.

The next step is to gather the information we need to perform our AMVR analysis. I recommend that plan participants and plan sponsors use five-year periods of annualized returns to analyze a fund's performance. The reason I recommend using five-year periods of return is to try to minimize the potential impact of any unusual periods, either positively or negatively, to ensure the reliability of the analysis.

Five-year periods have been shown to be generally more reliable in analyzing investment periods, as they often include a bear market or a market correction, and thus are a more complete picture of investment performance. If possible, rolling five-year annualized returns are an even better means of analyzing an investment's consistency and reliability.

In most cases, the most recent five-year annualized return for funds is provided by various publications and online services. Remember that the Active Management Value Ratio™ calculation requires the five-year annualized return for both the specific investment and its appropriate benchmark index fund. For plan sponsors and plan participants who decide to analyze additional five-year periods of annualized returns for a fund, there are several online calculators that can calculate annualized returns for a fund.

The other piece of information needed to compute a fund's Active Management Value Ratio™ is the annual expense ratio for both the fund being analyzed and its appropriate benchmark index fund. Although we use a fund's five-year annualized return in computing a fund's Active Management Value Ratio™, we can use the most current annual expense ratios for both the specific fund and the benchmark index fund, as it provides us with the most current data.

In many cases, the Active Management Value Ratio™ calculations are going to expose many funds as being extremely cost inefficient, and therefore eliminate such funds from consideration. For the funds that pass the Active Management Value Ratio™ review process, the next step is to calculate the correlation of returns for the available investment alternatives.

Having addressed cost efficiency, the next step is to address diversification, or more accurately, effective diversification. The easiest way to calculate the correlation of returns is to use the correlation function (CORR) provided in Microsoft Excel. Again, the goal is to construct a portfolio that combines assets that have a low, or even negative, correlation of return to each other so that gains in some investments will hopefully help offset losses in other assets. Unfortunately, most retirement plans are over-weighted in highly correlated equity-based mutual funds, making effective diversification a challenge.

ERISA requires that a retirement plan offer at least three investment alternative, with each investment alternative being diversified and having materially different risk and return characteristics.[2] The requirement of three diversified investments is done in order to provide plan participants with the opportunity to construct a retirement account portfolio that is both suitable in terms of a participant's financial profile and effectively diversified in order to minimize the risk of large losses in the participant's portfolio.

Historically, fixed-income investments, real estate related investments (e.g., real estate investment trusts, partnerships), and commodities (e.g., precious metals, oil) have proven to be reliable in effectively diversifying a portfolio. Most retirement plans only offer plan participants one fixed-income option as a diversification tool. While the inclusion of a real estate related investment option would offer more flexibility, the omission of a commodity related investment alternative is probably a wise choice given the volatility of the underlying materials.

Having constructed the retirement portfolio, the plan participant's work has just begun. We previously discussed three schools of thought regarding asset allocation, one taking a relatively passive approach (static asset allocation) and the other two taking a more active approach to asset allocation (tactical asset allocation and dynamic asset allocation).

With regard to static asset allocation, the Will Rogers quote at the beginning of chapter twelve perhaps said it best. Static asset allocation just seems to be too antiquated and ignores the proven cyclical nature of the stock market and the economy. Furthermore, the fact that static asset allocation relies heavily on the misinterpretation of the BHB study is also problematic.

An active approach to asset allocation seems to make more sense, particularly in light of the losses suffered by investors in the 2002-2002 and 2008 bear markets. Of the two active approaches to asset allocation, I favor the dynamic approach due to the fact that it is based upon responding to real, current conditions, whereas tactical asset allocation is based more on possibilities projected in market and economic forecasts. However, the decision to adopt an active approach to asset allocation should include the proviso, "with moderation."

Short term attempts to successfully time the stock market have been shown to be both difficult and costly. Active asset allocation based upon either an intermediate or long term perspective makes more sense and can be justified as a legitimate risk management strategy. Commonly used tools in active allocation include economic indicators, stock market indicators, and technical analysis indicators such as moving averages and price momentum indicators.

The power of dynamic asset allocation can be demonstrated by the following example. Prior to the 2000-2002 bear market, the price-earnings ratio on the Dow Jones Industrial Average index had risen to 42, well above its historical average, suggesting that the index was at a level that was both overpriced and unsustainable. The prudent investor, recognizing the situation, would have reduced their risk exposure and preserved their wealth by reallocating at least some of their assets to less risky investments.

Further support for the dynamic approach to asset allocation can be found from both Dr. William Sharpe, a Nobel laureate for his work in the area of investment management, and Benjamin Graham, often acknowledged as the father of modern investing. Both Sharpe[3] and Graham[4] stress the importance of monitoring current market and/or economic conditions and adjusting one's investment portfolio accordingly in order to minimize the risk of large losses.

While investors need to monitor their portfolios, it is equally important to avoid micro-managing a portfolio. In most cases, a quarterly review is sufficient. More frequent reviews could be indicated based on significant developments in either the stock market or the economy.

Plan participants often indicate that they are hesitant to make changes in their retirement account due to the tax implications of making such changes. This is undoubtedly one of the biggest mistakes plan participants make in managing their retirement accounts. 401(k), 403(b) and 457 plans, as well as IRAs, are tax-deferred retirement accounts. As such, actions taken within such accounts involving replacing or reallocating investments are generally tax-free.

There are numerous stories of plan participants who suffered life changing losses in their retirement accounts because they had supposedly not been informed or had been misled about the ability to make tax-free changes in the investments in their retirement account. Sadly, under the current rules, the only protection against such situations is to be proactive and either educate yourself or seek experienced and knowledgeable counsel.

Chapter Sixteen

Becoming an Investment Genius

Simplicity is the ultimate sophistication.
Leonardo de Vinci

Any intelligent fool can make things bigger, more complex
and more violent. It takes a touch of genius – and a lot of
courage – to move in the opposite direction.
Albert Einstein

There seems to be some perverse human characteristic
that likes to make things difficult.
Warren Buffett

I am often amazed how many times the solution to a problem is relatively simple and right in front of us. We currently have a retirement system that is so complex that plan providers are legally allowed to intentionally deceive both plan sponsors and plan participants by claiming to be fiduciaries to create the illusion of trust and honesty, and then violate that trust and pad both their pockets and the pockets of their employers by knowingly recommending investments that are not in either the plan's or the plan participants' best interests, often without any liability whatsoever.

We currently have a system where plan fiduciaries, who have a legal duty to act solely in the plan participants' best interests, contribute to this shameful situation by providing plan providers with access to plan participants in exchange for administrative and bookkeeping services to keep the plan sponsor's costs low, when the harm caused by the plan provider's actions often far out-weighs the costs the plan saved via the exchange.

We currently have a system where plan participants often suffer "paralysis by analysis" due the volume of investment-related materials provided to them or the sheer number of the investment alternatives presented to them. Even worse, as we have suggested, the data provided to plan participants is often not the information that plan participants really need in order to have a meaningful opportunity to make an informed decision, a right guaranteed for ERISA plan participants, and a right that every retirement plan participant should have.

And yet, the solution to all of these problems is both simple and right in front of us. I like to refer to the solutions as the 3-D 401(k) plan, the 3-D 403(b) plan, and the 3-D 457(b) plan.

ERISA section 404(c) requires that in order for a retirement plan to qualify as a 404(c) plan, the plan must provide a participant or beneficiary with an opportunity to choose from a broad range of investment alternatives. The "broad range of investment opportunities" requirement is met only if the available investment alternatives are sufficient to provide the participant or beneficiary with a reasonable opportunity to:

(a) Materially affect the potential return on amounts in his individual account with respect to which he is permitted to exercise control and the degree of risk to which such amounts are subject; and
(b) Choose from at least three investment alternatives:
   (1) Each of which is diversified;
   (2) Each of which has materially different risk and return characteristics;
   (3) Which in the aggregate enable the participant or beneficiary by choosing among them to achieve a portfolio with aggregate risk and return characteristics at any point within the range normally appropriate for the participant or beneficiary; and
   (4) Each of which when combined with investments in the other alternatives allows a participant to diversify their individual account so as to minimize the overall risk of a participant's or beneficiary's portfolio and the risk of large losses.[1]

So under ERISA section 404(c), a plan could arguably be ERISA compliant by simply offering just three diversified investment alternatives that, when combined, would allow a plan participant to effectively diversify their portfolio to protect against large losses. Under ERISA section 404(c), once a fiduciary prudently selects investment alternatives for a participant-directed plan and continues to monitor the alternatives chosen to ensure their suitability, the fiduciary is generally not liable for investment losses suffered by a plan participant.

A valid argument can be made that a plan consisting only of three diversified investment alternatives (3-D plan) would be in the best interests of both the plan and the plan participants. By limiting the number of investment alternatives and preventing "information overload," the plan might see an increase in participant participation, both in terms of the number of participants and the amount of contributions, which could in turn lead to improved employee morale and lower employee turnover. Limiting the number of investment alternatives could reduce the plan's overall cost of administering the plan, possibly even to the point that the plan could provide such services in-house.

Adopting a plan limited to three diversified investment alternatives could reduce the participants' overall investment costs, thereby increasing participants' returns, while still providing similar, if not better, investment returns than most current retirement plans, especially those that rely primarily on actively managed investments. Limiting the plan's investment alternatives would also make it less difficult for participants to manage their accounts.

Even if plan does not adopt the 3-D plan model, plan participants can attempt to create their own version of the model as long as their retirement plan offers investment alternatives within the plan that allows the participant to do so. Given the ease with which such investment alternatives could be included and the value that would be provided to plan participants in including such investment alternatives within a plan, plan participants could, and should, request that such investment alternatives be included in their plan's investment alternatives.

The simplicity of the 3-D plan model is one of its strengths. However, the proven performance of the model in terms of risk management and returns is even more impressive, leading Dr. Henry Markowitz, the father of MPT, to admit that he simply divided his own portfolio equally between a broad based equity index mutual fund and a broad based fixed-income mutual fund.[2]

Markowitz's 50 percent stock/50 percent model (the 50/50 model) finds further support from legendary investor Benjamin Graham. Graham suggested that the best portfolio for most investors might be a simple 50/50 split between stocks and bonds.[3] While admitting that the 50/50 model might not provide investors with optimal returns, Graham supported the 50/50 model due to its ability to provide both respectable returns and effective risk management for investors. Recognizing the potential value of active asset allocation and the ever changing nature of the stock market, Graham suggested that the allocation to either stocks or bonds never exceed 75 percent or, accordingly, be less than 25 percent.[4]

A review of the 50/50 model shows how the model can benefit plan participants. As previously noted, as the end of 1999, the price-earnings ratio on the Dow Jones Industrial Average index was 42, significantly higher that the index's historical average of the mid to high teens. Everything seemed to indicate that the market's level was both overvalued and unsustainable, and it was.

Over the next three years, the stock market averages suffered several losses. Using the Vanguard Total Stock Market Index fund and the Vanguard Total Bond Market Index fund, two low-cost index funds, as proxies for the stock and bond components of the 50/50 model, we can see how the model could have provided plan participants with both improved returns and greater risk protection.

Between 2000-2002, the Vanguard Total Stock Market Index fund suffered an annualized loss of 14.31 percent, with a standard deviation, or risk volatility measurement, of 18.99 percent. During the same period, Vanguard Total Bond Market Index fund had an annualized gain of 9.35 percent, with a standard deviation measurement of only 3.31 percent.

Had a plan participant used the 50/50 model using the two Vanguard funds during the 2000-2002 bear market, they would have only suffered an annualized loss of 1.06 percent, with a standard deviation measurement of 7.67 percent, approximately 60 percent less than a portfolio consisting of the Total Stock Market Index fund alone. Had a plan participant heeded the signal provided by the DJIA's overvalued price-earnings ratio, they could have possibly avoided a loss altogether and managed to achieve a positive annualized return over the same period.

There are those that might say the referenced example is meaningless, as no investor would allocate 100 percent of their portfolio in one type of investment. While such an allocation would be ill-advised, the example is still meaningful for several reasons.

First, funds such as the Total Stock Market Index Fund and other diversified mutual funds and ETFs provide an investor with exposure across various categories of the stock market. Without such diversification, the plan participant's loss could have been much larger. During the same 2000-2002 time period, the Standard & Poor's 500 Index, a large cap indicator, lost approximately 49 percent of its value, and the NASDAQ, a small cap indicator, lost approximately 78 percent of its value.

Second, the example demonstrates how easy it can be to construct and maintain a properly diversified, and yet inexpensive, retirement portfolio and avoid the cost inefficient and "closet index" investment alternatives commonly found in retirement plans. There are a number of mutual funds and exchange traded funds that provide the same cost efficient and effective diversification as the referenced Vanguard funds.

Plan sponsors and plan participants need to work together to build a mutually beneficial retirement plan that provides for and protects each other's best interests. The suggested 3-D plan model would be both easy to implement and easy to maintain, both from a compliance and a cost perspective.

As suggested by ERISA, the three investments could be as simple as a well diversified equity-based fund, a diversified fixed-income fund, and a money market fund, as both fixed income investments and cash historically have a low or negative correlation to equity-based investments. From the plan's perspective, the historical correlation of returns between the three would satisfy the plan fiduciary's duty of prudence, thereby reducing their potential liability exposure. The simplicity of the plan should also lead to reduced administrative costs, potentially even allowing for in-house provision of such services.

From the plan participant's perspective, the limited number of investment alternatives, as well as the correlation of returns between the investment alternatives, could make portfolio construction and maintenance easier for plan participants, potentially resulting in increased participant participation. The availability of investment alternatives such as low cost index mutual funds and exchange traded funds would reduce the impact that fund fees and expenses have on a plan participant's end return. Plan participants could also benefit from the relative simplicity that would be required in providing meaningful education programs.

Studies have shown that society is resistant to change. As the Einstein quote at the beginning of this chapter states, anyone can create and maintain a complex system, especially when it serves their own bests interests to do so. However ERISA mandates that plan sponsors and other plan fiduciaries must always put the interests of the plan participants and their beneficiaries first.

Whether a plan sponsor chooses to adopt the suggested 3-D plan model alone or as the core element of its retirement plan, a failure to consider the 3-D model and implement the model in some way has potential liability implications for plan fiduciaries given the model's potential cost and performance benefits for plan participants.

Chapter Seventeen

Managing Your Account

Only when the tide goes out do you discover who's been swimming naked.
Warren Buffett

Creating your retirement account portfolio is only the first step toward financial security. As the 2000-2002 and 2008 bear markets proved, investors need to implement effective risk management strategies to avoid "swimming naked," or being exposed to the risk of unnecessary financial losses.

Fortunately for investors, the internet has made it much easier for plan participants to monitor their retirement account portfolios. An online search for "stock charts" or "investment analysis" will direct you to the various online sites that can be used to monitor your portfolio.

The two primary approaches to investment analysis are fundamental analysis and technical analysis. Fundamental analysis is more appropriate for individual investments than it is for investments like mutual funds, as it uses profitability measurements such as profit margin, return on equity, and ratio analysis, e.g., price/earnings and price/sales, to assess an investment.

Technical analysis is more suitable for investments such as mutual funds. Technical analysis uses time-related measurements such as price momentum charts and moving averages to detect changes in the overall market or an investment.

In my practice, I use various technical analysis techniques to monitor both investments and the market, including moving averages, moving average convergence-divergence charts, average directional movement index charts, relative strength charts, money flow index charts, point-and-figure charts, Japanese candlestick charts, and three line break charts. However, plan participants do not need to use such an extensive list of techniques in order to protect their retirement account portfolio.

Moving averages are a relatively simple strategy that plan participants can use to monitor both their retirement account portfolio and the stock market in general. Moving averages are just what their name implies, an average that changes over time. Most online charting sites allow investors to compute two types of moving averages-a simple moving average, which assigns equal weights to each period being analyzed, and an exponential moving average, which assigns greater weight to the most recent period being analyzed.

While moving averages can be a helpful analytical strategy, there are potential drawbacks that plan participants should consider. While shorter time frames can be more responsive, they are also subject to "whipsaws," or false signals. Longer time frames are less prone to false signals, but less responsive.

Given these issues, many investors use a dual moving average technique to manage their investments. One common dual moving average strategy utilizes both a 50 period and a 200 period moving average. Signals can be as simple as a cross-over of the 50 period moving average above/below the 200 period moving average. When the 50 period moving average is above the 200 period moving average, that would be a favorable signal. When the 50 period moving average is below the 200 period moving average, that would be a unfavorable signal.

While technical analysis has been criticized as not being full-proof, the recent bear markets clearly illustrate the risks inherent in a buy-and-hold, or some would say a buy-forget-regret approach, as such an approach ignores the proven tendencies of the stock market. A buy-and hold approach to investing also ignores the value of risk management and the true impact of significant investment losses.

Chapter Eighteen

Retirement Rollovers and Transfers

Hopefully, upon reaching retirement, a plan participant will have to decide what to do with a large balance in their retirement account. Plan participants have basically three alternatives upon retirement: take a lump sum distribution, leave their money in the company's retirement plan, or transfer the money to an IRA or a Roth IRA.

Taking a lump sum distribution is generally not a smart decision as it would result in the entire balance being subject to immediate taxation. Leaving the money in the company's retirement plan is usually not a good idea due to the lack of flexibility in terms of investment choices and the fact that most corporate retirement plans do not allow plan participants to maximize tax deferral within the account by using the "stretch" strategy for their beneficiaries.

In most cases, the plan participant's best option is to transfer the balance in their retirement account into an IRA or a Roth IRA via a rollover or a direct trustee-to-trustee transfer. In a rollover, the plan participant actually takes possession of the funds in his retirement account. A rollover is generally a tax-free distribution and transfer of a plan participant's assets from one retirement plan to another retirement plan.

In a rollover, the plan participant has sixty days to establish another retirement account, usually an IRA or Roth IRA account, and deposit into the account an amount equal to the original balance in their retirement account, including any funds withheld by their employer at the time they withdrew their funds from their retirement plan. Employers are generally required to withhold 20 percent of any distribution that is paid directly to a plan participant. The requirement that a plan participant replace all funds withdrawn from their retirement account, including funds withheld by their employer, is a common rollover trap that is not always understood by plan participants.

Plan participants who fail to deposit the entire amount of the original balance in their retirement account into an IRA, Roth IRA or other qualifying retirement account within sixty days will generally face having the missing funds subject to immediate taxation as income and an additional 10 percent tax on the missing funds as an early distribution penalty unless the plan participant has reached the age of 59½ prior to the distribution, or qualifies for one of the various legal exceptions to the early distribution penalty.[1]

Under current ERISA law, all qualified plans are required to give plan participants the option of performing a direct rollover of their retirement account assets unless the rollover distributions are expected to total less than $200 for the year. My experience has been that many plan sponsors are not aware of this provision and may simply choose to provide the plan participant with a check for the proceeds from their retirement account, making the distribution subject to both the withholding trap and the early distribution penalty.

ERISA does not specifically require a plan to perform a trustee-to-trustee transfer on rollovers. Plan participants who wish to take advantage of the direct rollover rule should ask their plan sponsor to provide them with a check made out in such a way to document that the plan participant never took actual or constructive possession of the funds. The easiest way to accomplish this is to open up an IRA or Roth IRA account prior to requesting a rollover and to direct the plan sponsor to make the check payable to the new IRA custodian as custodian of the plan participant's IRA, e.g., No-Load Fund Company, as custodian of the John Doe IRA, Account No. 123456.

One last issue that deserves mentioning is transferring company stock within a retirement account. Company stock within a plan participant's retirement account often qualifies for special tax treatment as net unrealized appreciation if properly handled. If the company stock is rolled over or otherwise transferred to an IRA, the beneficial tax treatment may be lost. Plan participants with company stock in their retirement plan should contact a tax attorney prior to taking any action with regard to transferring the retirement account assets in order to preserve the potential tax benefits of net unrealized appreciation.

Plan participants should use the direct trustee-to-trustee transfer option whenever possible in order to avoid the withholding trap and to simplify the entire retirement account transfer process. A trustee-to-trustee transfer is not a rollover. As the name infers, in a direct trustee-to-trustee transfer the plan participant never takes either actual or constructive control of the funds in their retirement account. Since there is no distribution to the plan participant, the transfer is tax-free and the plan participant is not subject to either the 20 percent withholding rule or the 10 percent early distribution penalty.

An additional benefit to using the trustee-to-trustee transfer option is that a plan participant can make an unlimited number of annual trustee-to-trustee transfers. Generally, you can only make one tax-free rollover involving all or any portion of your retirement funds within a one year period.

The subject of retirement plan distributions and retirement plan rollovers/transfers is a highly specialized area of the law. The foregoing comments are in no way intended to be or are a complete discussion of all of the potential issues that should be considered by a plan participant before actually transferring the assets in their retirement account. Applicable laws and regulations are subject to change and every plan participant's situation is unique. Plan participants should always consult with an advisor who specializes in such matters prior to making any decisions or taking any action involving the assets in their retirement account.

Chapter Nineteen

Closing Argument

Facts do not cease to exist because they are ignored
Aldous Huxley

Men occasionally stumble over the truth, but most of them pick
themselves up and hurry off as if nothing had happened.
Winston Churchill

When I decided to write this book, I did so with two goals: (1) to provide useful, easy to understand information to alert both plan participants and plan sponsors to certain practices within the financial services/retirement investment industry to allow them to better protect their financial interests, and (2) to do so in a manner that could be read in a short period of time, as studies have shown that most people are more likely to read something that can be read in a short period of time. Hopefully, I have accomplished both goals.

A Schwab Institutional study estimated that approximately 75 percent of the investment portfolios they reviewed were unsuitable for the investors studied given the investors' financial goals and investment needs.[1] The industry's response to the Schwab study-"we've always known it."[2]

If a similar study were done of retirement portfolios within American 401(k), 430(b) and 457(b) retirement plans, I believe that the study would find an equal, or even higher, percentage of unsuitable portfolios. I believe that there are two primary reasons for the sad state of American retirement plans: (1) a failure to provide plan participants with sufficient information in order to allow them to make informed investment decisions; and (2) a failure to provide plan participants with investment alternatives that perform well in terms of both cost efficiency and performance.

While plan sponsors have expressed concern regarding the ability of their employees to effectively manage their individual retirement accounts, there is no legal requirement that plan sponsors provide investment education or investment advice to their employees. When plan sponsors do provide their employees with investment educational programs, the programs usually fail to provide meaningful information to the plan participants.

The problem with most retirement plan educational programs is that they are usually provided by the plan's service providers. The plan's providers simply lack the objectivity needed to provide the plan participants with all of the information that the plan participants need to make informed investment decisions. Plan providers certainly are not going to provide plan participants with any information regarding any problems or issues with the plan's investment alternatives.

While both the Department of Labor and the courts have consistently adopted the principles of Modern Portfolio Theory as the standard for determining whether plan sponsors have acted prudently in managing a retirement plan, there is no requirement that plan participants be provided with the correlation of returns for the investment alternatives within the plan, even thought factoring in the correlation of returns for investments is the cornerstone of Modern Portfolio Theory and plan sponsors should already have this information in order to fulfill their fiduciary duty of prudence.

Most retirement plans are over-weighted with equity-based investment alternatives, especially costly, actively managed mutual funds with poor performance records relative to index mutual funds. Costs matter, as a study by the Department of Labor estimated that over a twenty year period, each 1 percent of investment fees will reduce a plan participant's end return by approximately 17 percent.[3]

Studies have consistently shown that actively managed mutual funds underperform index mutual funds. And yet, despite the overwhelming evidence of the underperformance of actively managed mutual funds, many retirement plans limit their investment alternatives to actively managed mutual funds, much to the detriment of plan participants.

Variable annuities have numerous anti-investor attributes, most notably an inequitable inverse fee structure that is based on the accumulated value of the annuity owner's annuity rather than the annuity issuer's actual cost to provide the legal obligation called for by the annuity. Over time, the high fees and expenses associated with variable annuities, often in excess of 2 percent a year, can dramatically reduce a plan participant's end return. And yet some variable annuities are the preferred investment alternative, in some case the only investment alternative, of 403(b) plans.

As outlined herein, it would be easy for plan sponsors to simplify the entire retirement plan process in such a way as to be both ERISA compliant, cost-efficient and plan participant friendly – thus promoting a true win-win situation for everyone and staying true to the idea of "protecting and promoting the interests of plan beneficiaries and their beneficiaries" and providing plan participants with "sufficient information to make informed investment decisions. Hopefully, plan sponsors will consider doing so.

Notes

Chapter 1: A Curious Paradox
1. 29 U.S.C.A. § 1001(b) et seq.; In re Unisys Sav. Plan Litigation, 74 F.3d 420, 442 (3d. Cir 1996)
2. Available online at www.sec.gov/news/studies/2012/917-financial literacy-study-part1.pdf
3. 29 C.F.R. § 2550.404c-1(b)(2)(i)(B)
4. 29 C.F.R. §§ 2550.404a-1; 29 C.F.R. § 2509.96-1; Tittle v. Enron Corp., 284 F. Supp. 2d 511, 547-48 (S.D. Tex. 2003); DiFelice v. U.S. Airways, 497 F.3d 410, 423 (4th Cir. 2007)
5. Harry Markowiz, "Portfolio Selection: Efficient Diversification of Investments," 2d ed. (Wiley & Sons, 1991)

Chapter 2: Fiduciary Duties Under ERISA
1. Donovan v. Bierwirth, 680 F.2d 263, 271 n.8 (2d Cir.), cert denied, 459 U.S. 1069 (1982)
2. 29 U.S.C.A. § 1104(a)(1)(A), (B) and (C)

Chapter 3: A Battle of the Best Interests
1. Donovan v. Bierwirth, 680 F.2d 263, 271 n.8 (2d Cir.), cert. denied, 459 U.S. 1069 (1982)
2. Donovan v. Cunningham, 716 F.2d 1455, 1467 (5th Cir. 1983)
3. 29 C.F.R. § 2550.404a-5

Chapter 4: Fiduciary "Trickeration"
1. 29 C.F.R. § 3(21)(c)(1)(i) and (ii)
2. Urban Dictionary, available online at www.urbandictionary.com/define.php?term=trickeration

Chapter 5: Disclosure, Disclosure, Disclosure
1. 29 C.F.R. §§ 2550.404a-5(a), 2550.404c-1(b)(2)(i)(B)
2. 29 C.F.R. §§ 2520.104b-2, 2520.104b-10
3. 29 C.F.R. §§ 2550.404a-5(d)(1)i)(B)
4. 29 C.F.R. §§ 2550.404a-5(d)(1), 2550.404c-1(b)(2)

Chapter 6: "Sufficient Information to Make an Informed Decision"
1. Pension and Welfare Benefits Administration, "Study of 401(k) Plan Fees and Expenses," ("DOL Study"), available **at** www.DepartmentofLabor.gov/

ebsa/pdf/401krept.pdf; "Private Pensions: Changes Needed to Provide 401(k) Plan Participants and the Department of Labor Better Information on Fees."("GAO Study"), available online at www.gao.gov/ new.item/d0721.pdf, 7

Chapter 7: Countering Conflicts of Interest

1. John Bogle, *"The Little Book of Common Sense Investing: The Only Way to Guarantee Your Fair Share of Stock Market Returns,"* (John Wiley and Sons, 2007), 33
2. Charles Ellis, *"Winning the Loser's Game: Timeless Strategies for Successful Investing,"* 5th ed. (John Wiley and Sons, 2009), xii
3. Ellis, *Winning the Loser's Game*, 45
4. Standard & Poor's Indices Versus Active SPIVA® Scorecard, Year-End 2011, available online at us.spindices. com/documents/spiva-us-yearend2011.pdf (used with permission)
5. Ibid.
6. Ibid.

Chapter 9: Variable Annuities – The Most Overhyped, Most Oversold And Least Understood Investment Product in America
1. DOL Study and GAO Study
2. William Reichenstein, "Who Should Buy A Nonqualified Tax-Deferred Annuity," Financial Services Review, (Spring 2002), ; William Reichenstein, "An Analysis of Non-Qualified Tax-Deferred Annuities," Journal of Investing," (Summer 2000), 11-31; Richard B. Toolson, "Tax-Advantaged Investing: Comparing Variable Annuities and Mutual Funds," Journal of Accountancy, (May 1991), 71-77; William Bernstein, "A Limited Case for Variable Annuities," available online at www.efficientfrontier.com/ ef/701/annuity.htm
3. Reichenstein, "Who Should Buy."
4. Ibid.
5. Internal Revenue Code § 72(t)
6. Jeff Opdyke, "Shifting Annuities May Help Brokers More Than Investors," *The Wall Street Journal*, February 16, 2001, at Section C1.
7. Reichenstein, "Who Should Buy"

Chapter 10: Target-date Funds
1. 29 C.F.R. § 2550.404c-5(b), 5(e)
2. James Colon, The Problem With Target-Date Fund Glide Paths,"available

online at www.advisorperspectives.com/ newsletters12/9-targetdate3.php

Chapter 11: Risk Management – The Secret to Successful Investing
1. Charles Ellis, "*Winning the Loser's Game*," 22, 89-90
2. Javier Estrada, "Black Swans, Market Timing and the Dow," available online at www.iese.edu/jestrada/PDF/ Research/Refereed/BSMT Dow.pdf
3. Ibid.

Chapter 12: Asset Allocation
1. Gary P. Brinson, L. Randolph Hood and Gilbert L. Beebower, "Determinants of Portfolio Performance," *Financial Analysts Journal* (July/August 1986), 39-48

Chapter 14: The "Absolute" Truth About Successful Investing
1. Available online at www.sec.gov/news/studies/2012/ 917financial-literacy-study-part1.pdf
2. Mark Warshawsky, Mary DiCarlantonio and Lisa Mullan, "The Persistence of Morningstar Ratings", Journal of Financial Planning (September 2000), 110-121; Christopher Blake and Matthew Morey, "The Morningstar Mutual Fund Star Ratings: What Investors Should Know," http://www. tiaacref institute.org/ucm/groups/content/@ap ucm p tcp docs/documents/ document/tiaa02029412.pdf

Chapter 15: Putting It All Together
1. DOL Study and GAO Study
2. 29 U.S.C.A. § 404(c)-1(A), (B), and (C)
3. William F. Sharpe, *Investors and Markets: Portfolio Choices, Asset Prices and Investment Advice* (Princeton University Press, 2006), 207-208; William F. Sharpe, "Adaptive Asset Allocation Policies," *Financial Analysts Journal*, (May/June, 2010), 45-59
4. Benjamin Graham, Jason Zweig and Warren Buffett, "*The Intelligent Investor: The Definitive Book on Value Investing. A Book of Practical Counsel*," (Collins Business Books, 2003), 22, 89-90

Chapter 16: Becoming an Investment Genius
1. 29 C.F.R. § 2250.401c-1(b)(3)(i)(A)-(C)

2. Paul Farrell, *"The Lazy Person's Guide to Investing: A Book for Procrastinators, the Financially Challenged, and Everyone Who Worries About Dealing With Their Money,"* (Warner Business Books, 2004), 154, 157

3. Graham, Zweig and Buffett, "The Intelligent Investor," 22, 89-90

4. Ibid.

Chapter 17: Retirement Rollovers and Transfers
1. Internal Revenue Code § 72(t)

Chapter 19: Closing Argument
1. Brooke Southall, "Wirehouse accounts don't match client goals," *InvestmentNews*, March 12, 2007, 12

2. Ibid.

3. DOL Study and GAO Study

Appendix A

Recommended Reading

William Bernstein, *"The Intelligent Asset Allocator: How to Build Your Portfolio to Maximize Returns and Minimize Risk,"* (McGraw-Hill, 2000)

John Bogle, *"Common Sense on Mutual Funds,"* 10th ed., (John Wiley and Sons, 2010)

John Bogle, *"The Little Book of Common Sense Investing: The Only Way to Guarantee Your Fair Share of Stock Market Returns,"* (John Wiley and Sons, 2007)

Charles Ellis, *"Winning the Loser's Game: Timeless Strategies for Successful Investing,"* 5th ed., (John Wiley and Sons, 2009),

Benjamin Graham, Jason Zweig and Warren Buffett, *"The Intelligent Investor: The Definitive Book on Value Investing. A Book of Practical Counsel,"* (Collins Business Books, 2003)

Daniel R. Solin, *"The Smartest Portfolio You'll Ever Own,"* (Penguin Books, 2011)

About the Author

Mr. Watkins is an honors graduate of Georgia State University and a graduate of the University of Notre Dame Law School. He has also earned both the CERTIFIED FINANCIAL PLANNER™ designation and the ACCREDITED WEALTH MANAGEMENT ADVISOR ᔆᴹ designation from the College of Financial Planning.

Mr. Watkins is the Founder and CEO/Managing Member of InvestSense, LLC, an investment education firm that provides programs to individuals, pension plans, educational institutions and other groups on proven and effective wealth management strategies, including strategies for the accumulation, management, preservation/protection, distribution and recovery of wealth.

Mr. Watkins is also the owner of The Watkins Law Firm. He has been an attorney since 1981 and is a member of the Fiduciary Section of the State Bar of Georgia. His career also includes serving as a compliance official with several national brokerage firms and as the director of financial planning quality assurance for an international insurance corporation.

He has extensive experience in the areas of financial planning, asset protection, wealth management and preservation, forensic financial planning, fiduciary law, fiduciary oversight services, securities/investment law, estate planning and retirement planning.

Mr. Watkins is the owner of two blogs. "CommonSense InvestSense" (investsense.com) provides useful information to individual investors and fiduciaries on topics such as investments and wealth management. "The Prudent Investment Advisor Rules" (iainsight.wordpress.com) provides information on best practices for investment advisors and professional fiduciaries. He has been quoted in various publications and on various online sites.

Made in the USA
Lexington, KY
07 July 2013